Good Grief: Daily Meditations

A Book of Caring and Remembrance

D1569147

Praise for: Good Grief: Daily Meditations

Though your writings often make us cry, they say all the things it is hard for us to express. The pain of losing our son is almost unbearable at times, but it is comforting to know there is someone like you that truly understands. You have taken us one step further beyond grief.

Mark and Donna Vickers
for whom this book was written

Schoenbeck captures beautifully what I have heard others say about their grief, and what I have experienced myself. Her readers will be grateful to find their thoughts and feelings so accurately named and understood. *Good Grief's* abundant resources are a gift to all who face the death of someone they love. Schoenbeck's extensive experience as nurse and teacher, and her evident care for those who have known loss, make her eminently qualified to write about grief.

Kathleen Fischer
author of numerous books related to spiritual realms, including
Transforming Fire, Autumn Gospel, Women at the Well, and
Imaging Life After Death

Sue writes for all people irrespective of religious preference. Her writing is evocative and touching. She opens the doorway into a world of remembrance … a world we all may access any time we wish.

Father John Domin
Archdiocese of Portland

Good Grief: Daily Meditations

A Book of Caring and Remembrance

Susan L. Schoenbeck

DANCING MOON PRESS
NEWPORT, OREGON

Good Grief: Daily Meditations
A Book of Caring and Remembrance
copyright © 2011 by Susan L. Schoenbeck
All rights reserved

ISBN-13: 978-1-892076-84-7
Library of Congress Control Number: 2010942637
Manufactured in the United States of America

Schoenbeck, Susan L.
Good Grief: Daily Meditations —
A Book of Caring and Remembrance
1. Title; 2. Death; 3. Grief; 4. Meditation; 5. Health, Mind & Body; 6. Spiritual.

Book design: Carla Perry, Dancing Moon Press
Cover design & production: Dan Mandish

DANCING MOON PRESS
P.O. Box 832, Newport, OR 97365, 541-574-7708
www.dancingmoonpress.com
info@dancingmoonpress.com

FIRST EDITION

Contents

Preface

Good Grief: Daily Meditations
A Book of Caring and Remembrance

> We human beings tend to see ourselves primarily as
> physical beings. But we are not primarily a body
> housing a mind and a spirit. We are a spirit
> animating, for a time on this earth, a mind and a
> body. When our mind and body wear out and are
> gone, the spirit that is you and me remains.

It is not uncommon to ask when a loved one dies, "Why did this happen?" The person was good and kind, yet their death was painful or prolonged. We cannot make sense of this.

A disciple once asked a holy man why a child was born blind. The disciple questioned if the infant or parents had sinned and were being punished. The holy man allayed the disciple's fears, saying, "Neither this man nor his parents have sinned. But the works of a great spirit will be manifest in the child."

i

The holy man implied there may be a higher purpose to illness than we mortals can grasp. As in nature, disease and death come irrespective of moral or spiritual practices.

The human body is subject to many diseases and acts of man, nature, and beast. We all die of one or more of these causes. Our bodies are only the earthly forms of us.

Being deemed as "holy" does not separate one from the inevitable decline of the body. Buddha died from food poisoning. Saint Bernadette succumbed to cancer and tuberculosis. Pope John Paul the II suffered from end-stage Parkinson's disease. The famous diet guru Doctor Robert C. Atkins died from consequences of a slip and fall.

We all are susceptible to forces beyond our control. War has claimed our sons and daughters. Drugs have claimed our siblings and children. Persons with mental illness have fired shots that killed innocent bystanders.

We do not know the end of our own story … we do not know how or when death will come. Nor would we want our loved ones to worry about how we died. Instead, we give these words to those we left behind so they remember that death does not erase a relationship. Death only changes its format.

> *Today I will tell myself there is no answer to why my loved one died. There will never be an answer. I will no longer ruminate over the details. I will accept the death and go on, taking with me what I can from my loved one.*

This manuscript began on a series of index cards. A friend

had lost his son. In a sympathy card, I included three cards with thoughts relating to death learned throughout my nursing career. After three days, my friend returned and asked, "May I please have more of your cards? They helped me." So, I wrote more cards.

He returned a second time, saying, "My wife and I read your cards together. We'd love to read any others you might have." So again, I wrote more cards for my friend. Later he returned, saying, "Your cards mimic exactly what we are feeling. How do you know what we are feeling?" I continued writing.

This family, which lost a most precious son, used the cards as daily meditations. They shared with me the music their child had created. Inspired by his music, I listened to it as I wrote. A connection was made. I began to process the materials, including how the family was responding to the writings. By the anniversary of their son's death, I had written more than three hundred and sixty-five entries and they had all been read by the family.

At that point, my friend and I talked about the joy of remembrance, the passion of celebration—of inclusion, not exclusion—and the everlasting spirit of Evan Mathew Vickers, who was born on July 4, 1973 and died on October 15, 2005. Out of tragedy came hope and a renewed love.

These words were written in honor of
Evan Matthew Vickers

Introduction

This book is dedicated to those who have lost loved ones and whose hearts are broken. The thoughts and experiences contained in *Good Grief* are meant to soothe the pain of grief, which is unimaginable to those who have not experienced such loss.

Friends often gather at the time of death and then, as the weeks and months go by, they slip away. It's in our nature to find it more comfortable to attend a memorial service than to sit beside a friend who is experiencing their sixth month of grieving. We do not know what to say. Most often, we say nothing. This book lets people know they can help each other not feel so alone after losing a loved one.

For years, we have been told those who grieve should accept their loss and move on. But we are ill equipped to stop loving someone who has been important in our lives. This is something most of us cannot do. Our memories contradict the notion that the deceased does not exist anymore. We remember those who have passed on and experience them in our everyday lives with a sense of awe, connectedness, and joy.

This book shows us how we can continue expressing our love for them. We learn that awareness of the continuity of life after death opens the door to a continued relationship with a loved one.

Good Grief is meant to be read one day at a time. Readings in the beginning of the book focus on those universal feelings we all have soon after the death of a loved one. The book then leads one through readings that invite contemplation of immortality. A section on remembrance confirms that lost loved ones continue to be with us.

Most pages contained in *Good Grief* have three sections. The segment at the top of the page is a statement to help the reader think more expansively about death. The boxed section is an affirmation the reader may contemplate each day. The third section contains a quote that validates the mourners' feelings by letting them know they are not the only ones who feel the way they do. Progression through the three parts will lead readers to sort out truths and gain an awareness of the eternal spirit with whom they may commune.

May these words and thoughts inspire readers to remember lost loved ones and to pass down their stories and reaffirm that the love of family and friends is with us every day. Love, after all, never ceases.

Chapter One
Gifts of the Near-Death Event

This book is the voice of the dying telling us we can live more fully if we understand what dying is like.

Working with patients has taught me a lot about the process of dying. I'd like to share with you what I have learned from the stories of patients who have experienced a near-death event. What I have learned may help ease your pain and sorrow.

A near-death event is a spiritual experience of undetermined origin that happens at the time of clinical death or during an experience of grave physical or psychological danger. Near-death events happen to people young and old, rich and poor, religious and atheist, Buddhist, Christian, Muslim, and Jew.

Scientists, doctors, and nurses do not agree on what causes a person to experience a near-death event. Some say chemicals go haywire. Others believe lack of oxygen causes a person to hallucinate. One researcher proposed that the brain becomes short-circuited by random electrical impulses.

Whatever the cause of a near-death event, the important thing to remember is that people believe it happens and

1

their perception is their reality. People report the event with striking similarity. Near-death experiencers tell of being out of their bodies, hovering above the scenes where they crossed over. They say there is no pain once they are outside their bodies. Looking down from a point above the scene of their dying, they reveal that they can hear and see what is happening. As time goes on, near-death experiencers move through a tunnel into the presence of a light described as a compassionate "light-being." At this point, the person is asked questions such as, "What good did you do with your life?" "How did you love?" "When someone hurt your feelings, were you able to turn around and forgive that person?" "How did you help someone in need?" Those reporting near-death events said they reached a barrier and were told they were going no further. Some caught glimpses of a place beyond. They described it as beautiful and tranquil. There were some differences in describing the other side, as could be expected. What we see depends on who we are.

The near-death experiencers referenced in this book came back, of course. You may ask why. I believe they returned to tell us what dying is like so we can be at peace with the inevitability of death. Near-death experiencers agree there is no end to life. Their stories raise the question, "Are we dying or just moving on?"

A story or two will help you grasp the knowledge and wisdom a near-death event brings. It would be foolhardy not to prepare for the literal "adventure of a lifetime," so let us begin.

******

The first time I realized near-death events occurred was

after resuscitating a patient in a cardiovascular surgery ICU (Intensive-care Unit). I was a new graduate nurse. When Sally coded, I was the first to the bedside. I was nervous. Although I had seen CPR (Cardiopulmonary Resuscitation) enacted dozens of times while I was a student nurse, this was my first professional experience. I followed the protocol. Within minutes, Sally was okay. I was relieved. I stayed at her bedside to assess her. Then Sally began to tell me she had come back from "the tunnel." I probably looked puzzled, so Sally continued, "When my heart stopped, I could see you up on the bed doing CPR on my body. I saw you breathe for me. I saw you press down on my chest. But I was drawn into a tunnel that had a bright light at the end. The light seemed to call me to it. I looked back and you were working hard to revive me. Suddenly I found myself 'popped' back into my body. So here I am. Only when I came back could I feel the pressure of your hands. You are stronger than you think."

Do I ever wonder if Sally came back from the tunnel to help me out? I do. At first I thought she may have been so kind as to come back to get me out of a crisis. A pretty egocentric reason, you could say.

As the years progressed and I heard more and more stories from patients who claimed to have had near-death events, I wondered if Sally had come back to teach me a lesson. Her message was—there is no death—at least not like we think. Death according to Sally was a trip out of her body and away to a place where there was no pain. Sally awakened me to the process of listening to patients who had similar experiences.

******

When I was teaching about near-death event occurrences at a conference for emergency personnel, a physician approached me during a break in my talk. He said, "You've got it right. I know you have it right."

The doctor went on to draw a picture of what dying was like. He sketched a hospital room. He drew his body on the bed. Surrounding him was the CPR team that had responded when his heart stopped. The doctor worked at this hospital so he knew the faces of the people in the room. He penciled in a hazy form at one corner at ceiling height. This, he told me, was his spirit.

The good doctor said he could see and hear everything going on in the room from his spirit's vantage point. He said he had no pain, although he remembered being in pain after gall bladder surgery just prior to his cardiac arrest. He could not feel the nurses and doctors do compressions on his chest. He did not feel his head fall back as a doctor opened his airway to insert a tube. The only feeling he had was that of being drawn to a place out of the room by some unseen force. He was ready to go until his wife arrived.

This doctor's wife cried, "Harry! Please Harry, don't go." This was the first time during his cardiac arrest that he heard his name mentioned. The mysterious pull to leave was strong until the sudden call of his name by his wife brought him back. His spirit returned to his body.

The doctor had learned something quite important—it gave him a new picture of what dying was like. Now he knew people could watch and hear hospital staff. He realized that a loved one calling someone by name could be a turning point in a near-death event. He began to greet all his patients by name, putting names with faces ... just in case he would need to call them back one day.

******

I cared for Stan after his lawn mower accident. This sixty-eight-year-old gentleman had been riding too close to the edge of a hill when the machine tipped over, pinning one leg. Stan had spent several weeks in our hospital's rehab unit after undergoing many surgeries. He was in isolation due to a persistent wound infection.

Stan's heart stopped unexpectedly. There were no warning signs. We found him not breathing and without a pulse. After pressing a code button to alert other staff, we immediately started CPR. Stan made it through. We thought how lucky it was that we found him in time.

Stan thought otherwise. "Why didn't you let me go?" he asked. I didn't know how to respond. Stan continued, "I was out of my body and doing just fine until you nurses came along. For the first time in a very long time, I had no pain. You cannot imagine what that was like. But when you resuscitated me, I was pulled back into my body. I saw a place where my father, mother, and sister beckoned me. I wanted to go to them. I did not want to come back through the tunnel. Next time, let me go."

I learned a valuable lesson from Stan. Every nurse should know the resuscitation wishes of each patient. And every nurse should help patients talk openly about what they want.

******

Sarah was a nursing assistant who cared for Florence, a longtime resident of a nursing home. Florence had dementia and needed help bathing and dressing. Sarah worked the four-to-eight p.m. shift.

One evening, Sarah was wheeling Florence back to her room to help her retire. Sarah had made this journey with Florence many times before. Each time, Sarah would guide Florence through the steps of changing into her nightie and brushing her teeth ... but not this particular evening. At seven o'clock, Sarah wheeled Florence to the doorway of her room.

Florence pointed to the room across the hallway and spoke clearly, "Look at all the angels over there. I want to sit here and watch them." Sarah saw nothing across the hall. Sarah tried in vain to persuade Florence to go to bed so she could complete her work. But Florence stared at the ceiling across the hall and refused to go into her room.

The next day Sarah returned to work. There was a lot of loud talking and crying during the change-of-shift. A beloved patient had died the evening before. This patient had been found hanging from her bedrail by the ties of her gown. It was presumed she was trying to get out of bed but when her gown ties got tangled, she suffocated. Staff found her about nine o'clock in the evening. The woman who died had been a resident of the room directly across the hall from the room where Florence lived.

Sarah was quiet. She felt awkward. Should she share a story that she herself was not sure was true? The room quieted to absolute silence when Sarah told them what Florence had said the evening before.

Is anyone really alone when dying?

Probably not.

The Spirit's Journey

How does it feel to die? We mortals know some facts about the dying process. We have listened to the stories of people who have been clinically dead and then resuscitated. Modern medical miracles have provided us with more than a few storytellers. What is surprising is that in all cultures people of all religions report similar events happening to them when they died. Those who have returned from death tell of floating above their bodies and watching the scene below. When the departed were out of their bodies, all their pain was suspended. This aspect was a great joy for many who had considerable discomfort in life. People who journeyed out of their bodies when clinically dead said their anxieties were replaced by feelings of well-being and peace.

Some days it is the way you died that haunts me...
the dying part. I thought there must have been an
amount of pain—physical or psychological—that
was just too much for you to bear. So, you went on. I
am comforted by the stories of people who have died
only to return to life. I know now you did not suffer
in the end.

Are we here to laugh or cry?
Are we dying or just being born?

—**Herman Wouk,** *Winds of War*

From Dust To Dust

Doctors may pronounce you dead. Your body may be buried, or the dust from your bones sent off into the wind. Your spirit, however, remains, independent from your body.

> *Knowing that at death the spirit survives comforts me. This knowledge assures me that you and I will always be connected; I am keeping you on my mind and in my heart.*

There is no such thing as empty space.

—Linda Hogan in *Solar Storms*

Spiritual Existence

Eternity is mysterious. Eternity is not something that begins after you are dead. It is going on all the time. We are in it now. To think we change at death into forms of beings we cannot fully understand is perplexing, but true.

> *You are in my heart. I tell myself that you do still exist. I believe you exist as a spirit. I do not know how far my story on earth will go. But I will meet up with you. Until then, keep me in your heart. I would feel better knowing that you do.*

Keep me in your heart for a while.

—Warren Zevon, "The Wind"

Light

Ancients believed mortals merged at death with the rays of the sun spirit. This is comparable to modern day man's report that during a near-death event, a person who is declared clinically dead meets with a bright "being-like" light that gives unconditional love.

> *I am comforted knowing you are in a place of love.*
> *May you find the love of the Light.*

I weave light into words so that
When your mind holds them
Your eyes will relinquish their sadness,
Turn bright, a little brighter, giving to us
The way a candle does
To the dark.

—**Hafiz**, *The Gift*

Floating Above

People who experience near-death events report that they left their bodies, floated above them, and were led into a tunnel. At the end of the tunnel, they met up with deceased friends and relatives.

> *I want to knock on the doorway to heaven. I want to see that you are okay. Knowing people reunite after death comforts me.*

Only chance can speak to us.

—**Milan Kundera in**
The Unbearable Lightness of Being

Peace

People who experience near-death events say they were pain-free and peaceful when they crossed over to the other side. Even automobile accident victims and soldiers gravely injured on the battlefield say that, at the moment of clinical death, they left their bodies and floated without pain or anxiety above the accident or battle scene. For those who suffered much physical pain or psychological torment before the near-death event, the change was welcome and comforting.

> *I find comfort in knowing*
> *you had no pain at the end.*

Our hearts must know the world of reason and reason must be guided by an informed heart.

—**Bruno Bettelheim** in *The Informed Heart*

Unconditional Love

People whose hearts have stopped and then are restarted report that they went to a place where they felt unconditional love from a being of light. Some people have to die before experiencing such love for the first time.

> *You have always been a bright light. Please, now shine love on me. Illuminate my path.*

The experience of being loved by God enables us to accept our false self as it is, and then to let go of it and journey to our true self.

—Thomas Keating in *Open Mind, Open Heart*

The Other Side

People who survive CPR say they floated above the scene as medical staff did chest compressions. They say the pain they had once experienced was gone during this brief interval. Despite the commotion of healthcare workers frantically trying to save them, the person felt calm and peaceful. Survivors report they went down a tunnel and, at the end, met a being of light who greeted them with unconditional love. They also spoke with family and friends who met them on the other side.

> *I ask myself who was there to greet you. I wonder, "Which people met you and welcomed you?"*
> *I review this picture in my mind again and again.*
> *I can only guess who might have met you. But I am comforted to know you were taken care of when you arrived.*

The family, not the individual, is the real molecule of society, the key link in the social chain of being.

—**Robert Nisbet** in *The Twilight of Authority*

Wisdom

Deaths are beautiful experiences for the dying, even if those deaths come about due to prolonged illness, military battle, or accidents. We can only imagine the beauty that people who return from death say is beyond description. Death is not painful. People leave in peace with the lightness of being. The grace of the Great Spirit is evident within the death experience.

> *I keep having flashbacks to the time you died. I, at first, thought dying must have been painful. Now I have learned that you actually floated out of your body when you died. I understand you did not feel pain as you left. For this, I am grateful. I am taking my memory of your death and attaching new pictures because I have learned what the process of dying is like. I gave up my faith in God when you were taken. But now, I am looking for God again.*

It was a wise man who invented God.

—Plato

Taking A Piece Out

Grieving takes a lifetime. Parents who have lost children say they feel as if a piece of them has been cut out, leaving a gaping wound that never really heals.

> *I am working on understanding death. My understanding that death is a beautiful experience helps some. I hope my dreams about your death become less about how it happened and more about memories of the good times we shared.*

I want to know God's thoughts.
The rest are details.

—**Albert Einstein**

Luminous

People who have been over to the other side during clinical death describe the love of God as luminous, compassionate, and unconditional in giving. The thought of such a divine being gives mankind hope. And it is this hopefulness that gets us through the bad times.

> *Your death is too much to understand. I can only hope that what people say is true … that I will be reunited with you.*

He who made us
Must surely love us
His reason for ordaining death
As the final act of life
Must, therefore,
Be somehow connected
With his love.

—Omar Khayyam Stanza 62 in *The Rubáiyát*
Explained by Paramahansa Yogananda

Being Of Light

It is common to hear a person who has experienced clinical death, such as in cardiac arrest, say "I met a Being of Light who loved me unconditionally."

> *I am comforted knowing that death is a place where love is.*

And I saw that the lines of light led not to a realm but to a being and that the light and hook were his, and that they were made of love alone.

—David James Duncan in *The River Why*

Eternity

Eternity does not begin at death. You are in it now. There is a worldly side of you and an eternal side of you. You can focus your attention here or there.

> *I am waiting here. Will you cross over and come to me?*

We are not human beings having a spiritual experience; we are spiritual beings having a human experience.

—Wayne W. Dyer, M.D.

Never Say Good-bye

One lesson we learn from people who have been clinically dead and revived is that we really never need to say "good-bye." "So long" would be more appropriate. When we die, we meet up with loved ones on the other side.

> *I am sure you will meet me.*

You live on earth only for a few short years, which you call incarnation, and then you leave your body as an outworn dress and go for refreshment to your true home in the spirit.

—**White Eagle**

No Words

Those who have been resuscitated have a hard time putting into words what they experienced on the other side. Suddenly, they had knowledge and peace that went beyond human understanding. Those who returned to life after clinical death said they were enveloped by a light that seemed like a being of unconditional love. They did not need to use words to understand what others were thinking. Neither languages nor colors nor religions separated them.

> *I suspect you can see me from the other world.*
> *I guess you understand what I cannot truly grasp.*
> *I suspect the peace that is beyond my understanding*
> *is now yours.*

If you are not afraid of death, the universe becomes a friendly enough place ... it is a great paradox, but making death more attractive as the near-death experience does ... makes life more attractive.

—Bruce Greyson, M.D.

Existence Beyond Death

When watching a person die, we might say, "This death is a blessing." We mean that we are pleased this person is no longer in pain. We hope the person transitions to a better place. Once the person is pronounced dead, most people end their conversations. We do not talk to people who have died. We know that people float above their bodies and look down at the scene below when they cross over into clinical death. The dead see what is going on. We know that dying people hear what is happening around them. How odd is it that we behave as if the person who has died cannot see and hear us. It is as if we truly believe they no longer exist.

> *Sometimes I am hesitant to tell others that I talk to you. Because you are gone, many people don't say your name anymore. I am the odd duck. I am a little frightened to walk alone on this path with you. I cannot say too much to other people for fear they will think me crazy. They do not believe me when I say you are both here and there.*

Death ... is no more than passing from one room into another. But there's a difference for me, you know. Because in the other room, I shall be able to see.

—Helen Keller

Messages of Water

In the book, *The Hidden Messages of Water*, Dr. **Masaru Emoto** tells us that music affects water. Harmonious music enables water to form beautiful crystals that do not form when non-melodious music is played. Adult bodies are approximately 80 percent water. An interesting question: "Does music affect the fluids that run through our bodies and, also, our very spirit?"

> *I like to surround myself with the music you loved.*
> *Something good happens inside me when I hear your*
> *music. It is like you are beside me once again.*

The most visible creators
I know are those artists
Whose medium is life
Itself. The ones who
Express the inexpressible
Without brush, hammer,
Clay or guitar.

They neither paint nor sculpt.
Their medium is being.
Whatever their presence
Touches has increased life.

They see and don't have to draw
They are the artists of being alive.

—Jane Stone

Remembered Forever

Some believe that death is the final chapter. The book is finished. *C'est finis*. Others believe that when people die they go on to a different level of existence. Some believe people may come back in a different life form. Others believe no one is truly dead as long as the person is remembered by someone.

> *Before you died, I never thought about saying "good-bye" to you. I live for that first "hello" when we meet up again. There is no end to my love for you. You are remembered and loved each day.*

*Just as a little bird
Cracks open the shell
And flies out, we fly out
Of this shell, the shell
Of the body. We call
That death, but strictly
Speaking, death is nothing
But a change of form.*

—Sri. S. Satchidananda in Bill and Judy Guggenheim's
Hello From Heaven

Overlapping Worlds

Birth and death are moments when time and space overlap.

> *I search for you wherever you are. I call out to you to come back to me. Sometimes I feel your strength enter my veins. Sometimes I hear your voice beckon in my words. I know the dead can visit the living, for I have felt your presence here beside me many times.*

*Faith dares the soul to go farther
than it can see.*

—William Clarke

A Glimpse

We can only imagine the afterlife. Until we are finally set free from our bodies, a glimpse is all we get.

> *I used to worry about heaven and hell. Now I give thought to neither. I sense you are all right wherever you are. You have given signs you are okay ... just somewhere else. My heart understands there is peace in the grave.*

Conventional knowledge tells us that we are separate; higher wisdom informs us that we are one. A shift of perception reveals that we are all the same consciousness, manifesting in different bodies, the way leaves are part of the same tree.

—**Dan Millman** in *The Laws of the Spirit: Simple, Powerful Truths for Making Life Work*

Letting Go

Death is inescapable.

> *Every day I pray that God grant me the strength to accept your death. I am not afraid to join you when my time comes, because I feel you are somewhere safe.*

Some think it's holding on that makes one strong; sometimes it's letting go.

—Sylvia Robinson

The Truth

Death is the end of life, or so we have been taught. Such narrow thinking can cloud our seeing beyond the veil of this life into the next. Knowledge can be truth, or a barrier to truth. Throughout life, we must question what is true.

> *Nurses tell me they see and hear people talk to people on the other side just before they die. I believe the nurses when they say we can communicate between worlds. I sit here and wait and listen for your presence. Knowing you are just beyond comforts me.*

The truth lies closer to what we feel in our hearts rather than what we think in our minds because the truth has not yet been contaminated by self-doubt, self-consciousness and fear.

—Carl Hammerschlag

Encounters

Encounters with death may enhance understanding of body and soul. Before experiencing the death of a loved one, people often think that "soul" is that part of a person that survives death. However, soul is not a separate part created precisely when we cross over to the other side. Rather, soul is the essence of who we are during life, and later, during death.

> *I used to be limited in personal insight and understanding of the soul because I was preoccupied with my body. No one ever taught me soul awareness. Now I see that my body is just a vehicle in which I go along preparing my soul for the light at the end of the tunnel of life.*

It is only when we truly know and understand that we have a limited time on earth ... and have no way of knowing when our time is up, that we will begin to live each day to the fullest—as if it were the only one we had.

—Elisabeth Kübler-Ross, M.D.

Away From Pain

People can leave their bodies during acute episodes of pain. The person may float above their body and feel no pain.

> *I am consoled that you were not in pain at the end.*
> *For this I am thankful.*

She learnt me how the Indian bears pain.
He lets his body mind go to sleep
and with his spirit mind,
he moves out of the body and sees the pain
instead of feeling the pain.

—**Forrest Carter in** *The Education of Little Tree*

Chapter Two
Communication Before and After Death

We cannot flee death. It will find us no matter where we hide. Even after someone has died, that person may contact us. This chapter looks at how we can embrace death and enjoy interactions with our loved ones who have died.

Before: Deathbed Talks

The willing suspension of disbelief unveils a new world. Until I became a nurse, I did not know what a person was like when approaching the end of their life. Because I had been trained as an intensive care nurse, I was alert at all times for signs I would need to perform CPR. After I witnessed dying numerous times, I concluded that death is not always a sudden occurrence. In many cases, death is preceded by recognizable events. I came to understand that no one dies alone.

The terminally ill often predict with firmness and accuracy their death is coming. We professionals, despite all our technology, are often surprised when the final crisis actually arrives. The dying often say that they see and talk to people who have died before. If you listen, you will come to know how people talk to loved ones on the other side as they themselves are making plans to leave their bodies. Nurses often find dying patients talking to someone they cannot see. Usually, the patient looks up to a corner of the ceiling of the room to carry on this conversation. The nurse may catch phrases such as, "I see you there and I will join you soon." "I am not ready to come." "Yes, I will follow the light."

And the patient may respond to the nurse by saying, "I see the angels on the bench. They are waiting for me. I must go." "I am waiting for the train." "I see the horsemen coming." The dying say they see and hear spirits who have come to guide them into another existence.

You will find nurses charting in the clinical record, "Patient says he was in heaven today and talked to family who had died. He seems happy to tell me this. He is in and out of being oriented to place and time. He talks to people who are not present. Plan to check frequently for hallucinations."

If you look at the medical records of these patients, don't be surprised that the documented "hallucinations" occurred in the twenty-four-hour period before they died.

Several recurring themes emerge from deathbed talks:
- Focusing attention on the corner of a room at ceiling height.
- Being in the presence of the dead and angels. For example, "Mom and pop are here with me," or "The angels are waiting for me."
- Preparing for, and later ready to travel, saying for example, "I'll be ready soon. I'm coming."
- Being in another world and stating, "I see the light. It is so beautiful."

- Being able to control time of death. For example, the dying person asking, "What day is it?" in order to die on the date they choose.
- Becoming lucid one last time.

When I was a Coronary Care nurse, I had a patient who knew better than I that death was coming. Lora, a patient with chest pain, was admitted to an ICU bed where I worked. She was hooked up to a monitor that displayed her heart rate and rhythm on a monitor. She had an intravenous line inserted in case she needed emergency drugs. We were running the usual battery of tests to confirm the suspected diagnosis. Nothing seemed unusual to me at the time.

One night shift, I noticed Lora was not sleeping. At 2:30 a.m., I went into her room, checked her blood pressure, and asked her how she was feeling. She calmly asked if I could arrange for her to be given communion. Her words were polite. She was alert. She looked me in the eyes and reached out her hand to mine when she asked me to call the priest.

I phoned the priest on call. Father Mike was seventy-three-years-old but never missed morning rounds to offer communion. "Tell her I will be there in the morning," he said.

"But, she wants you to come now," I said.

There was silence on the other end of the phone and then, "But she's not on the seriously ill list, is she?"

I knew Lora wasn't, but I did not want to admit this. "I just put her on the SI list," were the words that came from my mouth, surprising even me.

"Okay, I'll be over," Father Mike conceded.

Lora received communion at 3:30 a.m. She smiled and

slept fine afterward. At 6:30 a.m. her heart stopped.

The autopsy later showed her ventricle had ruptured. No amount of CPR or emergency medications could bring her back. She died.

Reviewing the deathbed scene and putting things together, I look back at the time I was Lora's nurse. I am happy she had her last wish. I am not happy that I subjected her to all the resuscitation methods I knew. I started CPR. I led the team that gave her cardiac drugs from the emergency cart. I see now, although I did not see then, that she knew she was going to leave. She left on her own terms ... after taking communion.

******

My own mother had been sick for years. Her heart and lungs were failing after fifty years of smoking. She had been teased into smoking by the girls who hawked free cigarettes to office workers. She told me the cigarettes came in packs of three ... just enough to get you hooked. The public did not know then that cigarettes carried with them a death sentence for the smoker and those who breathed in the exhaled smoke.

In the end, my mother readied herself to leave. She gave away her belongings. She told me to take her picnic basket, something she prized. She gave me her favorite paperweight, a gift from a student from Thailand. A brass Buddha bell sits on my desk, another gift my mother received from a student.

I was living a hundred miles away, but my dad called to say he thought I should come home, as my mother was sick. I kept a packed suitcase in the car for such emergencies. I told him I just had to change clothes and get in the car. The phone rang again before I could leave. It was my mother. "I don't want you to come this time."

"What do you mean?" I asked.

"I mean I want you to wait. Your brother had to carry me up the stairs today after I had my blood drawn. I am not going to stand for that. I am telling you to not come."

My mother had always taken on the caregiver role. She had been experiencing bouts in which the room spun and she could not take control of her body. She wanted to be in control. She did not like being the one cared for.

My mother was taken to the hospital the next day and I met my dad there. Mother looked so small in the bed. I bet she weighed less than eighty pounds. We talked. She had me get her what she needed — her favorite nightgown. As we talked, she looked over at my dad who had fallen asleep. As dusk came, my mother looked at me and said, "Wake your father up and take him home. He needs his rest." This caring for everyone else was so like my mother. It was her way of being in the world ... always there for others. I woke my dad and told him I would take him home. We said our good-byes and that we would be back in the morning. My dad wanted to stop at a restroom. I took him and told him to wait for me there when he was done.

Then I followed a strong urge to go back to my mother's side. I could not leave just yet. When I got into the room, she smiled. I took her small body in my arms and cried, "Momma, I love you so much."

She said while hugging me, "I know you do. I love you too. Now go."

I took my father home. We got a call that night from the hospital. My mother had died. Did I regret leaving when she asked me to? No, I did not. I wanted my mother to have death the way she wanted it. She wanted me taking care of my father as she passed on.

******

Working as a director of nursing in nursing homes allowed time for me to meet and talk with staff. When a patient was close to death, we would discuss if anyone heard the patient talking to someone not present. We became good at listening for the clues that someone was planning to die. When patients looked up at the corners of their rooms and smiled, and talked to people not present, we were happy because we knew they were happy.

I was not surprised when a nursing assistant came to me on a Monday morning and excitedly exclaimed, "I knew 'Mr. Smith' was going to die. I heard him talking to the air and looking at the ceiling. He seemed happy. I called the family and told them he was talking to someone. They came to see him. He died the next day." Everyone has the opportunity to understand that people never die alone.

A Cat's Intuition

The dying are not the only ones who know when people are crossing over. Brown University reported about a cat named Oscar who lives in a dementia unit at a nursing home. Oscar cuddles up with patients who are going to die. The cat predicts deaths with 100 percent accuracy. When the staff moves Oscar outside the room of a dying patient, Oscar meows to get back in.

After Death: Communication

More than half the widows and widowers say they have seen, felt or otherwise been aware of the presence of their deceased spouse. Parents tell me they have been contacted by their beloved child who died. These are not out-of-the-ordinary folks. These are everyday people. Those left behind relay their stories to those who will listen.

Let me share with you a few stories that illustrate instances of the deceased contacting the living.

Cheryl was in her thirties. It was the time of the Vietnam conflict and her brother, Neal, was a pilot flying choppers to rescue the injured. Cheryl continually worried about Neal's safety.

This night, however, she was deeply engrossed in a novel. With only a chapter to go, Cheryl bid her husband "good night" and stayed up in a recliner, reading. In the middle of the night, Cheryl awoke. She sensed someone had come into in her house. She made sure the doors were locked. She opened closets. She even looked under the bed before she lay down next to her husband. The feeling was so real. Yet she was not scared. She just felt as though someone was watching her. "How silly," she told herself.

Cheryl slept in the next morning. Her husband woke her at noon asking her to take a call from her father. Cheryl got out of bed and grabbed the phone, expecting something to be wrong. Her dad had never called her before; her mom was the communicator in the family.

The news was sad. Men in uniform had come up to her parents' door. People with children serving in the military know what that means. Neal's helicopter had crashed. There were no survivors.

Cheryl spent the next few days on automatic pilot,

helping her parents do what no parent is ever ready to do: bury their child. Military personnel came to the funeral. There was a luncheon afterward in the church basement.

Cheryl didn't especially want to talk to her brother's army buddies, but one guy sought out Cheryl. "You need to know," he said, "Neal regarded you very highly. He told us guys that no woman was better than his sister. He felt you were the person to whom he was closest. We expected him back at base. When there was no communication, we knew he went down."

"When was that?" Cheryl asked.

"About zero eight hundred, military time," the soldier replied.

Cheryl figured out the difference in hours, with the time-zone changes, from the time her brother died to the time she awoke sensing the presence of someone watching her. It was the same time. Cheryl believes her brother stopped to see her one last time on his journey.

******

Paula is a nurse who loves her profession. She tries not to bring her patients' stories home. She believes in living a balanced life. Paula had been working with the dying on a hospice unit for many years when she was contacted by one of her deceased patients.

"I cared for Joan since she arrived on our unit," Paula explained. "We all knew there was nothing more we could do but comfort her. Joan had no hope for recovery and little time left. Both Joan and I loved the Beatles, so we'd sing the old songs together, not caring how we sounded. We talked a lot about Joan's life, her dreams, and what was to come next. We did the little things that count in life

... like having vanilla ice cream piled high with hot fudge sauce in the afternoon. We enjoyed each other's company. But, it still surprised me when I smelled her scent at my house. I was just doing little household chores when a scent I knew to be Joan's came out of nowhere. It would not have been so significant except that when I next reported to work, I discovered that Joan had died at the same time that the scent came to me at my home. I believe Joan stopped by on her way."

******

Mel was a nurse who worked with me on a fast-paced rehabilitation unit. Her son, Alex, already grown, came home for the weekend. Sitting at dinner with Mel and her husband, Alex said he came home for a reason. He said he was dying. Alex explained all the medications, even the experimental ones, he had tried. "No, no, no," Mel cried. "This cannot be."

But Alex went quickly. His parents were not with him the night he died. Instead, his brother, who slept in a recliner beside Alex in the hospital, came and spoke the dreaded words, "Alex is dead." Unable to console herself, Mel sat in the kitchen with a cold cup of tea. The phone rang. Mel answered it. No one was there. She warmed her tea. Fifteen minutes later the phone rang again. Mel answered it. No one was there. After finishing the tea, Mel "putzed" around, folding napkins and straightening a drawer or two. The phone rang. Mel answered it. No one was there. Mel found herself wanting the phone to ring because each time it rang, Mel felt like Alex was contacting her. Mel felt silly. She climbed into bed. She could hear the phone ring again as she fell into restless sleep.

Relationship

Many people say they knew a loved one died before they were actually told of the loved one's death. They say they had a feeling that the deceased visited them. A person's disembodied spirit may temporarily abide after death in an ethereal body that can communicate with the living.

> When I was told of the circumstances of your death,
> I thought back and discovered I was thinking of you
> at the time. Something made me aware of you.
> Death cannot erase our relationship.

Relationship is not a project; it is a grace.

—**Thomas Moore in** *Soul Mates*

A Part Of Me Still

Death makes us question. Death makes us cry. Experiences with death haunt some people. Thoughts of death frighten others. Death often does not give us enough warning to recompose ourselves to living without the departed. When someone dies, we fall apart. Rituals may focus on the deceased, but in so many ways, death is about the person who grieves.

> *When you stopped living, you did not leave me. Like sunlight weaving its way through trees and casting shadows of the leaves on the ground, I see your shadow in my day. There is no day without your presence. If I talk to you a lot, do not be surprised. You are a part of me still. We are inextricably intertwined.*

Rituals restore equilibrium.

—Jane Howard in *Families*

After Death Communication

After death, communications with a loved one are commonplace. Famed psychologist Carl Jung reported communicating with his deceased father.

> *There are those who tell me it is my imagination, fired by longing that makes me think I can still talk to you. Once in a while I meet someone who believes my contact with you is real and that communication with someone who has died is not a mystical phenomenon known only to me.*

Six weeks after his death, my father appeared to me in a dream ... It was an unforgettable experience, and it forced me for the first time to think about life after death.

—Carl G. Jung

The Widowed

Approximately 57 percent of the widowed say their deceased spouses appear and talk to them. Some widows and widowers report feeling touched by the person who has gone over to the other side. More than 70 percent of parents who have lost a child believe their deceased child has contacted them. Even people who are not related by blood or marriage say they have had contact with someone they knew after that person died.

> *I am no longer surprised when you make it known you are near me. Death has not erased our love and communication.*

An after-death communication (called an ADC) is a spiritual experience that occurs when someone is contacted directly and spontaneously by a deceased family member or friend.

—Bill and Judy Guggenheim in *Hello From Heaven*

Ordinary Reality

Ordinary reality is made up of daily life on earth. Non-ordinary reality is what happens where the edges of life and death meet, often called the "betwixt and between." It is important to understand that any person can reach into non-ordinary reality. You don't need to be of a specific religion to meet and honor spirits beyond life. You don't need to be a saint. You just need an understanding and the willingness to follow where your vision leads you.

> *Talking to you on a daily basis has made me aware of the betwixt-and-between worlds. It is in this space I feel your presence. I know that others may not acknowledge this non-ordinary reality where we meet. Nevertheless, the place we meet exists for us.*

It is the ability to think thoughts other than our own, other than the past, other than the safe, other than the acceptable that will lead us eventually to truth.

—Joan Chittister, OSB, in
Wisdom Distilled from the Daily

I Wish I Knew

People who are gravely ill and know they may die soon often try to talk to us about it. Our human nature, however, often makes us scared to talk about death and so we change the subject to something more pleasant. We give false reassurances to the person. We lie and say the person looks good. We assure the person not to worry. Our deceit impedes the dying from sharing their true feelings. Truthful dialogue ends.

> *Looking back, it was hard for me to face your death. Overwhelmed, I talked of trivial, superficial things. I wish I had just listened to you. The silence is so deafening now. I wish I had just listened to what mattered.*

Facts do not cease to exist because they are ignored.

—**Aldous Huxley, in** *Proper Studies*

The Presence Of Spirit

Because psychic phenomena attract so many people who are not in touch with reality, it is common for usually wise persons to cast it aside as unreal. But this is not always the case. We can communicate with people in other worlds without words.

> *I believe you are in a world out there beyond life on earth. I can tell people think I am being unreal when I say I can be with you still. I am both in touch with the everyday world around me, and also open to communication from beyond this life.*

You can kill the body but not the spirit.

—**Robert Louis Stevenson**

Facing Memories

Death reminds us that human life has its seasons, like nature—from pollination to the flower bud, from unfurled leaf to fallen leaves. When we are young, we reach out and touch and learn who we are and what reality is. We enter a phase wherein we feel we can conquer every challenge. We feel invincible, even facing death. As we age, we settle, raise families, and make our roots in communities. And then, before we know it, we have less time to look forward to than to look back. Looking back becomes a pastime filled with memories—some good, some bad. And we ask ourselves if we pursued life the best we could, using the kindest means.

I know that if I had to do it over, I would have been more kind to you. I always wanted to be kind. But stress, my tiredness, my aches got in the way of always being the person I wanted you to know me as. Know now that even if I wasn't the best, I tried my best because I love you. If I had another moment with you, I would tell you so.

We need energy, commitment, and courage not to run from our life nor to cover it over with any philosophy—material or spiritual. We need a worrisome heart that lets us face our lives directly, our pains, and limitations, our joys and possibilities.

—Jack Kornfield in *A Path With Heart*

Grace: The Tendering Of Our Memories

Nothing is as pure as it seems. Everything is influenced by who we are. We cannot look back and see what we saw before just as it was because we mix what *was* with what has happened since. Our mind adds and blends memories. Oftentimes, we see the departed nostalgically, with virtues that may belie reality. Our minds mix the many memories of our deceased loved ones, dropping out the bad memories. We know this tendering of our memory as "grace."

> *Yesterday. All my visions of you yesterday. I think of you and me. I replay memories in my mind. I revel in our closeness. I have faith the cord between us cannot be severed by death or time.*

Learning does not always take place at the moment you think it will. Learning may be a sorting out of data and drawing of conclusions at a later date.

—John Dewey

Opening Ourselves To Spiritual Encounters

Many things in this world are hidden. Einstein said there are emanations that man cannot see or understand. Our mind can take us places only if we let it. This process of opening ourselves to what we cannot see is like a man who hears someone knocking on his door. The visitor can enter only if the man will let him in. So it is with thoughts. By opening our hearts and minds, we can give that which may otherwise be inconceivable a chance to enter into us.

I feel that even in your non-being, you can be with me. In silence, I feel your presence with me.

Great spirits have always encountered opposition from mediocre minds.

—**Albert Einstein**

Separating Ourselves From This Busy World

The world is full of opposites. Sounds and silence. Being and non-being. For some, security is found only when sound and activity surround them. For these people, security is embedded in activity and noise. Silence may bring unsettling angst and anxiety. Disconnecting from this heavily jammed world, however, may be the only way to recognize the lightness of non-beings present all around us. Those who grieve are often comforted by friends who take quiet walks with them.

> *I sometimes seek out busy activity so I do not think of you. At times, your death weighs too heavily and I do not want to feel it. So I go where there are people who will not remind me of you. Other times, I want to take a quiet walk to be with you, and this is comforting. I am energized by this contact with your presence.*

When you appreciate the beauty and uniqueness of things, you rescue energy.

—**James Redfield** in *The Celestine Prophecy*

Our Connection

Relationships in this lifetime do not cease to exist once the body turns to dust. People continue to feel the spiritual connections of their souls.

> *You may be outside my view, but not outside my reach. Although I cannot see you, you are not gone. We are connected always. You and me, we will meet on the other side.*

I think we're both inside of another being we have created called "us."

—**Robert James Waller** in *Bridges of Madison County*

Death Rubs Me Raw

Death may strike unannounced. Death can pierce us with such force that we feel like a chunk of ourselves has suddenly been gouged out.

> *I have the blues. My heart aches raw. My memories, however, console me. So, I take time each day to think of the good times we had together.*

Life is what happens to you when you're making other plans.

—Betty Talmadge

Footprints

People may share their bodies. People may share their souls. People sometimes realize too late that they wish they had shared more. People go on as if there will always be time together. But we can never count on living one more day.

> *I am happy I felt your magic, your special being. No one can take from me what we shared. I wish there had been more time. But I am grateful we had time together. No one can remove the lasting impression you made on my life. Despite my sadness, I am happy you were here with me.*

My life is perfect because I accept it as it is.

—Lenny Kravitz, in "Eleutheria"

Returning

Ancients believed that people, once on the other side, had mystical powers. The deceased were thought to be able to go to earth during the day and return at night to the other side. Egyptians knew death not as annihilation, but as a transition to another form of existence wherein the deceased could contact the living.

> *My heart and mind reach out to you. You come to me. Once again our love is near. I feel your touch. Come often to me. I am waiting for you.*

They can because they think they can.

—Virgil

Messages Of Birds

Ancients thought that the deceased could take on the form of birds. Etruscan priests would observe birds outside the temple for messages from the Great Spirit. A girl in California died at home. The next day a bird appeared to her parents at the place in the house of the girl's death. The message of the bird was, "I am all right, just in another form."

> *I am always looking for you. Are you present in the bird whose gaze catches my eye? I stare at the bird with wonder. I am always looking for you.*

Perhaps the only limitations to the human mind are those we believe in.

—Willis W. Harman in *Global Mind Change*

Following Our Own Dreams

Thoughts. Ideas. Habits. Urges. We choose to follow our own dreams. We are anxious to touch the stars.

> *My mind races over the forks in the road of your life. You made decisions to go your own way. Everybody does. I did not always agree with your choices, but who am I to judge?*

You have to accept whatever comes and the only important thing is that you meet it with courage and with the best you have to give.

—Eleanor Roosevelt

Are We alone?

During the times we are alone, the presence of the deceased can be felt if we are willing to be touched. In silence we often find connection and peace.

> *Some days the sun doesn't shine. But, when I whisper your name, I hear your voice echo back from the clouds. And I am consoled.*

What a lovely surprise to finally discover how unlonely being alone can be.

—Ellen Burstyn

Measuring Others

Many measure people's lives by what they have achieved. But that is not the whole story. We also need to understand to what they aspired.

> *We did not agree on all things. Who does? But we loved so many of the same things. At times, when I am doing something we did together, I look over my shoulder because, for a moment, I think you are there.*

Endeavor to be patient in hearing the defects of others, of what sort so ever they be; for thou thyself hast many failings which must be borne by others.

—Thomas à Kempis, German Mystic

Enough Stuff

Many people strive their whole lives to gain money and the things money can buy. For them, nothing is enough. Success is measured by excess.

> *There is nothing I would not give to be with you again. I thank God that I have memories of the good times we shared. These memories are like precious gems to me.*

We seem to be working more than we wish and living lives that are less than they should be, to consume goods and services that we don't really want. For increasing numbers, the activities and goals of today's work conflict with their hopes for a better way of life, which seems possible, but ever elusive.

—**Fred Best in** *The Future of Work*

Where You Are

Time and space are mankind's invention.

> *Once you entered my heart, I did not give you a passageway out. Instead, I have always kept a place for you inside my heart. In this space we can meet to remember us, our times and our happiness. Come often to your place in my heart. I am waiting for you.*

I am always running into peoples' unconscious.

—Marilyn Monroe

Reaching You

We see things around us we know we should not touch—
a hot stove, an electrical wire downed by a storm, an open
wound.

Other things draw us to them—a baby's chubby toes, a
dog's furry face, petals from a daisy.

Sometimes we are touched by phenomena we cannot
see—heart-warming words that melt our hearts, a good
memory savored far beyond the time it was experienced, a
thought saved for the day it inspires us to action.

> *I tried to think of when I touched you last. I think of
> times you reached out to me with your hand. I repeat
> things you said to me. I hear your words in my mind.
> You and I are much more than meet the eye.*

*I can be separate from you only because at a
deeper level we are joined in something
inseparable. I cannot be alone alone.*

—James P. Carse in *Breakfast at the Victory:
The Mysticism of Ordinary Life*

Staying With You

Touch occurs on various levels. It can be physical. It can be mental. Through touch we connect. Without touch, we wither and die.

Touch can extend beyond our physical bodies and minds, beyond our physical packaging and beyond words. After all, we are more than a body. That we may not always recognize when and how we are responding to the various forms of touch in our world does not negate the fact that we are constantly being touched.

Allowing ourselves to be touched gives us a better understanding of our spirits. Understanding the depth and breadth of our ability to touch others opens us up to a new avenue for spiritual connection. We take in messages and we send out messages. We are all transmitters.

> *I am learning to live without you physically here. I still feel you near. You still remain. My hurting heart sends this message to you. Stay with me. Stay with me through my end.*

Certain thoughts are prayers. There are moments when, whatever the attitude of the body, the soul is on its knees.

—Victor Hugo

In Solitude I Find You

If there is one reason for death, it is to help us understand life.

> *Here I am, disengaged from the traffic of worldly existence. In silence, I seek not answers but just some peace of mind. I rest in a place neither here nor there—a place that seems closer to you.*
> *In stillness, I find you.*

Solitude is as needful to the imagination as society is wholesome for the character.

—James Russell Lowell in *Dryden*

Understanding

We learn some of life's lessons by going through bad times. We don't choose these situations. They choose us. We all experience sorrow.

> I know I may have misunderstood some of what you did in your life. And there are many people who do not understand why I do what I do. What is important for you to know is that our misunderstandings are inconsequential when I look at our relationship. It doesn't matter who was right or who was wrong. What matters most is that we experienced the mystery of life on earth together. This forever binds us together.

When a person has a real friend, he learns not only to appreciate another human being but he also learns to better understand himself.

—Susan Polis Schutz

Keeping Pace

Keeping pace on the technological speedway leaves people little time to reflect on their day or draw from their actions a picture of who they are and what they are doing on earth. Life is meant to be a journey we travel to get to know ourselves and our relationship to all things. Hectic lives breed people who have not taken the time to know themselves or others. In our quest for material gain and social status, it is easy to become estranged from our very selves.

How I wish I could spend some quiet time with you. Just an ordinary day with you would be extraordinary. I see now what I did not see before. Life is about people and their relationships. I feel you supporting me now as I stumble through my grief and learn to know myself better.

They're simply repeating the only behavior they know that will numb the mind and keep away the anxiety that comes from the lostness they feel.

—James Redfield in
The Tenth Insight: Holding the Vision

Qualities That Last Forever

Honesty. Love. Goodness. Fairness. We know these qualities to be real even though they have no physical form.

> *I am happy to have loved you. I still appreciate that you were honest and good. Your goodness remains indelible forever.*

You are the person in your baby pictures, you remember your eighteenth birthday, and you look forward to retirement. But this can only be the case if there is something that remains the same throughout your whole life, not something material, but immaterial. This enduring immaterial reality that makes you the same person throughout your whole life is your soul.

—Matt Koschmann in
Evidence for the Existence of the Soul

In The Moment

We find it hard in this busy world to be fully present in the moment. Society tells us we should multitask. Our worldview does not teach us the value of cultivating moments of quiet reflection. Guilt prevents us from just being. We must ask ourselves, "When have we allowed ourselves to be?"

> *I find myself alone in thought. I reflect on life. I remember you. I am in a prayer-like state of being. Nothing of the outside world matters. Only my primal connection to the universe matters. And in this state I feel your presence surround me with love.*

I see a shift in consciousness happening for the first time in more than just a few individuals here and there. It is a shift that the ancient teachers such as Buddha and Jesus pointed to — a possibility of living in a different state of consciousness.

—Eckhart Tolle in "Beyond Happiness and Unhappiness," *The Sun*, July 2002

Learning

Learning to accept other people unconditionally takes discipline. You have to put aside your emotions. You accept people for who they are despite the fact that you many not condone their behavior. The practice of unconditional love not only reframes our view of people, but also changes us. We become more open to whatever life holds.

> *Your spark showed when you said, "You better like me just the way I am." You were not going to change for anyone. I can respect that. It takes guts to be the person you choose to be. I miss you.*

Experience can only teach you what you are willing to learn.

—Beth Mende Conny in *Pearls of Wisdom*

Interwoven Stories

Our own story is interwoven with the lives of our loved ones who died. Thinking back on old times takes us back to them.

> *When I happened to think of a time long ago, you came into my mind. You are here now because of our past life together.*

I feel comforted knowing we are all in this puzzle together, knowing we are all just learning.

—**Kimberly Blaeser, Minnesota Chippewa, in**
Dreaming History: A Collection of Wisconsin Native American Writing

69

Keeping You To Myself

It is important we learn to vary our response to the circumstances in which we find ourselves. Sometimes we reveal much about ourselves. At other times, we hold back. It is okay to be choosy with whom we share our most intimate selves.

> *The people I just met never knew you. They can't tell by looking at me that there's a big chunk missing. Shall I tell them? I might. Not telling them does not expose my hurt. I may keep your life and my grief a secret from them.*

You may not feel like getting up, feel like trying to smile, or feel like making small talk. That's understandable.

—**Barbara LesStrang** in
After Loss: Learning How to Cope with Grief

70

Our Intentions

All relationships have a sense of intentionality. We make it known to another person that we want to be their friend. We want to have a relationship. So it is with connections to those who have died.

When we sit in silence and contemplate, we find that recollections of our loved one bring us feelings of comfort.

> _Only since your death have I sat alone thinking in silence. When the TV is off and the humdrum of the day silenced, I think you may be with me. This may be nothing else but my wish to have a relationship with you still. But it helps me._

Happiness is a conscious choice, not an automatic response.

—Mildred Barthel

Self-knowledge

As the day ends, we can leave the clatter of the world, and, in quiet, face ourselves.

> Sometimes I find myself thinking of you and me. You are a part of me still.

Self-knowledge is for the purpose of contributing. You change your perception of the past to bring peace to your present and our future.

—Jennifer James in
Success is the Quality of Your Journey

Connecting

Connectedness is something we cannot live without. We can live without TV. We can live without cell phones. We can toss away our iPODs. But we only truly live when we connect with one another. Connectedness is the quiet force that nurtures life in this irrational, irreverent, over-scheduled world.

> *There are times when I just need to separate myself from the chaotic day and be alone with you. It is clear to me that my daily acts of remembering you are really one of the blessings of my life. When I connect with you, I feel whole.*

The spiritual journey consists of the individual learning to recognize the self that lies within.

—Vedantā Uttarā Mīmasāmā in
Sacred Scriptures of India

Wherever You Are

The world is not as vast as the soul. The soul is truly without bounds.

> *I have loved you in this world. I love you still,*
> *wherever you are.*

There is No Death

I am standing on the seashore. A ship at my side spreads her white sails to the morning breeze and starts for the blue ocean. She is an object of beauty and strength and I stand and watch her until at length she is a speck of white cloud just where the sea and sky come to mingle with each other.

Then someone at my side says, "There! She's gone." Gone where? Gone from my sight, that is all. She is just as large in mast and hull and spar as she was when she left my side, and she is just as able to bear her load of living weight to her destined harbor.

Her diminished size is in me, not in her. And just at the moment when someone at my side says, "There! She's gone," there are other eyes watching her coming and other voices ready to take up the glad shout, "There she comes!"

And that is dying.

—An adaptation of Henry Jackson van Dyke's
A Parable of Immortality

Giving And Receiving

Each of us has been created as a spirit. When our bodies and minds wear out and are gone, our spirit—our gestalt—remains. The penultimate lesson of this life is to know how to give and receive love. Love spans both worlds. Love never ceases.

> *People say I am spending too much time thinking of you. Who are they to say my study of the spiritual is wrong? The spirit world seemed so abstract to me before you died. But now that you are there, I am very interested in learning about it. I have a place in me that glows with loving memories of you. This ember of love sustains me and will never die.*

I feel the capacity to care is the thing which gives life its deepest significance.

—Pablo Casals

A Mother's Presence

Prophet Khalil Gibran said, "Show me your mother's face and I will tell you who you are." A mother's love never falters. A woman knows her child's presence forever. Every mother and child ride up and down and all around on the carousel of time.

> *Your presence is seen in the family you left behind. When I see your smile on one of their faces, I know you are here also.*

My mother died six years ago on the full moon day of October. The midnight moon is as gentle and wondrous as a mother's love. For the first four years after she died, I felt like an orphan. Then one night, she came to me in a dream, and from that moment on, I no longer felt her death as a loss. I understood that she had never died, but that my sorrow was based on an illusion. I realized that my mother's birth and death were concepts not truths. The reality of my mother was beyond birth or death. She did not exist because of birth nor cease to exist because of death.

—Thich Nhat Hanh in *Fragrant Palm Leaves, Journals 1962-1966*

Music & Our Soul

Music remains with a listener long after the song ends. Music is a set of vibrations that affects our very soul. When the song is done, the feeling it brings stays in our heart.

I hear the music you loved. Sometimes I find myself humming a tune we shared. And it is like you have come home.

Music will haul you through a lot of stuff.

— **Georgia Ray in Martha Gies'** *Up All Night*

Growing Young

If we can understand that life is the foundation for death and an entrance to another life, then we can rejoice. If we learn to open our hearts and minds the way a child does —without the pretentiousness that society and advancing age often cultivate—we will see the light.

> *Thank you for being so easy to love. Thank you for giving me love. Love appears to be the eternal part of a relationship. For this, I am grateful.*

It takes a long while to grow young.

—**Pablo Picasso**

Meaning

We pursue life's meaning. No life would be well-lived without taking time to take stock. We ask ourselves, "What will happen to me when death's darkness comes?"

> *You lit up my life in so many ways. I imagine you as a candle whose light cannot be dimmed. I ask myself, "Why you? Why then?" There are no answers. I can only hope that when my time of death comes, you will be beside me to light the way.*

It is man's privilege not only to live but to be aware of himself as a living being and to explore the meaning of life.

—T. A. Kantonen in *Life After Death*

The Path

The poet D. H. Lawrence wrote that the good die young. Many older people ruminate over why a young person lived for only a short time. In learning to understand ourselves better, it is important to ponder what our relationships were with the deceased.

> *I have often thought you found peace. You knew who you were and didn't try to hide from anyone. You loved intensely. You gave profusely. And now I must figure out what our relationship meant.*

We must let our relationships reveal themselves to us.

—**Shakti Gawain** in *Living in the Light: A Guide to Personal and Planetary Transformation*

Moved by Music

In the eighteenth century, physicist Ernst Chladni showed how sand placed on steel discs scattered when violin music was played.

> *I play the music you loved again and again. The beat, the words, and the meaning touch me, and I feel your presence beside me once more.*

One good thing about music: When it hits you, you feel no pain.

—Bob Marley

I Seize You

Some people think their love for the deceased can only be shown by fretfulness and angst. These people do not enjoy good memories of the loved one lost. Suffering becomes the only way they feel connected to the departed.

> *I know that you would tell me to seize the day. You would not want me to wallow in anger or self-pity. I tell myself to enjoy life. You would wish me to do so.*

There is a loneliness that can be rocked. Arms crossed, knees drawn up; holding, holding on, this motion, unlike a ship's, soothes and contains the rocker. It's an inside kind—wrapped tight like skin. Then there is loneliness that roams. No rocking can hold it down. It is alive, on its own.

—Toni Morrison in *Beloved*

Awakened

Death brings a new level of awareness to us. We reach the understanding that time on earth is a limited part of our lifetime.

> *Your death awakened me. Before, I thought only about my day-to-day existence. Now I am trying to become a spirit you would be proud to know.*

A mind that is stretched by a new idea never returns to its original dimension.

—Oliver Wendell Holmes

Feeling Love

Thoughts have energy. We know when someone loves us. We feel the love.

> *My love for you has grown since your death. I admire the person you were even more today than when you were alive. In my thoughts, I honor you.*

The consciousness of one person can affect the physical substrate of another.

—Delores Krieger in *Therapeutic Touch*

Knowing Love

Strength and comfort are common elements of those who know they are loved.

> *Even though we are separated, knowing that you loved me helps me through each day.*

Our deeper understanding tells us that a truly evolved being is one that values others more than it values itself, and that values love more than the physical world and what is in it.

—Gary Zukav in *The Seat of the Soul*

Making A Print

Some people die quickly. Others slip gradually from our arms. Some folks are able to say good-bye. Other spirits pass back through life and give their loved ones a sign that they are okay on their way to the other side.

> *Just after you died, I lay awake in bed. My phone rang. I could hear no one there. I placed the phone back on the nightstand next to my bed. Again the phone rang. I could hear no one there. I have wondered if on this night you called to say good-bye.*

What was important was the golden footprint, the magic footprint she had left on his life and no one could ever remove.

—**Milan Kundera** in *The Unbearable Lightness of Being*

Choosing To Remember You

Religion talks about the presence of beings of another world. But in everyday life, most people do not talk about the dead. We seldom seek the company of the dead.

> I've spent a lot of time with religion and it has consoled me. I am comforted knowing there are a lot of people who understand that a spirit continues to exist after death of the body. I am conscious of your existence every day.

There is a part of you that is in the world but not of the world.

—Jesus

Stumbling Upon Wisdom

Love is stronger than death. We can love the spirit of a person while they are alive and continue to love this spirit after the loved one dies.

> *I am conscious of your presence in my life. I often think of what you would want me to do when I am facing a troubling situation. I have come to realize that your love for me will never die. Your guidance has a place in this life of mine.*

Where you stumble, there lies your treasure.

—Joseph Campbell

You Are A Happiness Inside Me

The people who are most important to us in life become part of our psyche. We are who we are, in part, because of them.

> *After your death, I caught myself singing a tune both you and I liked. I had to smile. My sadness was made sweet. Because of you, I became happy. I passed this happiness on to others also willing to pick themselves up and be joyful.*

This is the true joy in life, being used for a purpose recognized by yourself as a mighty one. Being a force of nature instead of a feverish, selfish little clod of ailments and grievances complaining that the world will not devote itself to making you happy.

—George Bernard Shaw

Relationship

When someone we love dies, we wonder if we communicated our love to the person. We have doubts. We can never assume people know we love them unless our actions show unconditional love. People know love not from words but from deeds.

> I ask myself over and over, "Did I share my love with you as much as I could?" I don't know. I say to you now that I love you. I hope you can hear me.

Death ends a life. But it does not end a relationship.

—Gene Hackman in playwright Robert Anderson's
I Never Sang For My Father

Awareness Of You

When someone we love dies, our relationship with that person does not end. It changes. The person becomes part of our mind, heart, and spirit.

> _I know you are there. Isn't it funny how your presence is felt even after your death? You are remembered by many people. You continue as part of our lives._

For we are the local embodiment of a cosmos grown to self-awareness.

—**Carl Sagan**

Walking With Me

Memory of a loved one lost to death is a sign that the one you love still walks with you wherever you go.

> *I know that people with whom I work have no idea how many times I think of you throughout the day. People who have lost someone dear to them understand. But others have no idea that you influence me today.*

I have felt a presence that disturbs me with the joy of elevated thoughts.

—William Wordsworth

Looking Forward

Human consciousness extends beyond the temporal gates we have been educated to perceive as real time. We are capable of recognizing the invisible, which knows no time parameters.

> *It took me a while to understand that I could look beyond this world to where you are. Although you are not here in my time, I can feel your existence in a parallel time. This helps me put my life into perspective. Now I know, when before your death I did not, that the life I have now is one in which I should build my character, for it is that which I will take onward into the next life.*

As I look back on my painful times, I see how much I have learned from the very situations that I immediately wanted to toss out of my life.

—Joyce Rupp in
Little Pieces of Light: Darkness and Personal Growth

Known By Kindness And Goodness

In our culture, we are often categorized by our occupation. Death of a loved one can elevate our consciousness to recognize that we are not just what we do. Rather, while we are doing what we do, we are developing the spirit of who we are.

> *I no longer identify myself by what I do for my work. Your death has made me realize that I am more than the everyday job by which this world defines me. I have discovered that I am a spirit known by my acts of love and kindness. The rest doesn't matter as much.*

Be grateful as your deeds become less and less associated with your name, as your feet ever more lightly tread the earth.

—Dag Hammarskjöld

Growing Stronger

Life seems to occur on two levels. One is our human life. The other is our spiritual existence.

> *If my thoughts could be seen, you would see love. Your death has led me to understand that love drives what I do and who I am. I have made a conscious decision to replace any anger and hate in my heart with love. I do this every day to honor your memory.*

Life breaks us all sometimes, but some grow strong at broken places.

—Ernest Hemingway

One Stick, Two Sticks

Siblings share more genes with each other than with either parent. The bond is genetic and real. It is important we hang with our siblings and share our likeness of being.

> *Certain melodies remind me of you: the cadence of your voice, the way you walked, how you glanced away when you were embarrassed, and how you held your head to the side when you looked in my eyes. All these familiar memories bring you close to me again.*

An Old Story

At the time of an old man's dying, he calls together his family. He gives a short, sturdy stick to each of his many offspring and relatives. The old man says, "Break the stick." Each person breaks their stick. The old man pronounces, "This is how it is when a soul is alone in the world without anyone. The person can easily be broken."

Next the old man passes out other sticks to each person and says, "This is how I would like you to live after I pass on. Tie your sticks together in bundles of two, three and four. Then try to break the bundles in half like you did the sticks."

No one could break the sticks when they were bundled together. The old man smiled and declared, "We are strong when we stand with other souls. When we are supported by others, we cannot be broken."

Our Individual Circumstances

We readily picture in our minds the size, shape, color, and build of peoples' bodies. It is harder to visualize their souls. Spirits are imageless.

> *Since your death I take a deeper look at people and try to see a person's spirit. I am coming to know myself and others by the qualities of their spirits. Be they kind. Be they compassionate. Be they greedy. Be they self-centered. Be they strong. Be they weak. Your death has taught me to look beyond the size, shape, color, and build to the true self, the imageless spirit. For that is who we eternally are.*

The more you judge others by your own standards, the more you show total disregard for their circumstances.

—Al Neuharth in *Confessions of an SOB*

Consciousness

Consciousness survives the body. We become an eternal presence. Religions refer to this consciousness as the spirit or soul.

> *I know that you were not destroyed by your death. I feel your presence. Sometimes a song makes me think only of you. Your face flashes in my mind. And we are together once more.*

Religions are different roads converging upon the same spot. What does it matter that we take different roads as long as we reach the same goal? And we are all struggling along the rocky, thorny road of the desert to reach God.

—Gandhi

Approaching Reality

The point of death is to teach us the transience of life.

> *I look backward and I see you younger. I remember you as you were then. I wonder if you are looking at me. Are you seeing me as I struggle to get through the day? Do you know what tomorrow will bring? Are you a light to show me the way?*

We can observe and theorize, but we can never know. Reality is something we can only approach.

—Albert Einstein

Thinking Outside The Box

Once there was a rich man whose house caught fire. The man yelled to his children, "Run, run, get out! The house is on fire!" The children were absorbed in their play and did not listen. The man thought, What can I do to get them to run out? He ran out of the house and yelled to his children, "Come out here. I have new toys and books for you." The children ran out of the house and the man was thankful.

> *Most days we must act serious about what we are doing in our lives. We have to act grown-up. No pretending. Some people think you are only here in my imagination. They don't get it. You are here. I learned to think "outside the box." And this has saved me.*

There was that law of life, so cruel and so just that one must grow or else pay more for remaining the same.

—Norman Mailer

Seeing Ourselves Through Others

Parents love all their children. But their love is expressed with special tenderness toward a child in need.

> *You had more burdens than I realized. It was difficult for me to understand this. Now I look back and realize that what I thought was true was not. What I hoped was false, was real. God teaches not just through words, but also through lives.*

We do not assume that our schedule is our own to manage, but allow it to be arranged by God.

—Dietrich Bonhoeffer in *Life Together*

In Our Hearts And Minds

It is a mistake to believe that people completely disappear. Although we become attached to how people appear, spirit forms are the essential nature of humans.

> *Like an alluring mirage, I am drawn to pictures of you. I flip through snapshots and remember times we shared. I am both overjoyed by the remembrances so sweet and dear and also saddened by the distance now between us.*

The dead rise and walk about the timeless fields of thought.

—Wendell Berry in *That Distant Land*

102

Everlasting Ways Of Being

The world's religions tell us that bodies are transformed at death. And that the essential nature of the person goes on as constant and changeless.

> The permanent you is who you really are. I think of what you stood for and who you intended to be. It is that person I seek in the quiet hours of the night when I cannot sleep and cannot stop thinking of you.

But you teach about him (Abraham Lincoln) like a dead man ... why don't you say he is still alive today in the hearts of your people?

—Kent Nerburn in *Neither Wolf Nor Dog*

Hidden Away

There was a man who fell asleep in a drunken stupor. His friend slept beside him until the next morning when he had to return home to herd his sheep. Just before leaving, the friend took from his bag some money and placed it in the lining of the drunken man's coat. When the drunken man awoke, he found his friend gone. He did not know of the money hidden in the lining of his coat, so he wandered about hungry and begging. A month or so later, the drunken man met his friend in the street. The friend said, "Why do you beg? I left you enough money to care for your needs for a long while." The man replied, "The money was hidden. I only saw my hunger and thirst."

Before you took leave, you gave me indelible impressions of your presence. Hidden away in me are the priceless memories I have of you. These memories can never be taken from me, and comfort me daily just as bread and water.

May the Sun Father and the Moon Mother shed their softest beams on you ... and upon those with whom you share your heart and home.

—**Coahuila Indian**

My Space, My Time

In life, we try hard to succeed. Through possessions and accomplishments, we try to show others who we are. In the end, we must give up all pretenses and prepare to leave our bodies behind, and to be who we have become on life's journey.

> *So my friends are out partying tonight. And I am here ... once again talking to you at your graveside.*

Seek balance and space, and solitude.

—**Loreena McKennitt**

Doing

You might as well stop trying to fit square pegs into round holes. Things are as they are.

I have told everyone I will start to go out. I have told everyone I will begin to celebrate again. I have told everyone I am ready. I'm okay. So I am tearing myself away from you tonight. Please help me.

The best form of saying is doing.

—**Jose Marti in Ernesto 'Che' Guevara's**
The Motorcycle Diaries

Consciousness

Some day each one of us will belong only to memory. We will be unseen but alive.

> *You are alive in my memories. I see you as you were. But more importantly, I feel you are somewhere safe. We come together in a holy reality known well by you and me. Through our contacts, I sustain myself and get new energy to continue.*

It is becoming more and more evident that consciousness survives the body. Therefore, the more clearly we shall understand ourselves as consciousness, the less afraid we shall be of dying.

—Thomas Hora, M.D., in
Beyond the Dream: Awakening to Reality

Choosing Our Way Of Life

Sitting Bull declared, "Let us put our minds together and see what kind of life we can make for our children."

> Like an echo of your spirit, I care for the ones whom you loved. I know you are here, giving me the strength and wisdom to do so.

It is up to us to determine whether the years ahead will be for humankind a curse or a blessing. We always must remember that it is given to men and women to choose life and living, not death and destruction.

—Elie Wiesel

Doing Good

Do the dead know if we have kept our promises? Probably so, it seems. We have all had moments when we've gotten an eerie feeling when being tempted to do wrong. We change our action and instead do right because we would not want to embarrass a deceased loved one.

> *When I make a promise to someone you loved and I feel you, in the spirit world, looking over my shoulder, I know it is up to me to do the things you would want me to do. I want to honor you by my deeds. I feel you behind me smiling approvingly, and this makes me glad.*

Just before dawn, a young man jogged along a deserted stretch of beach. In the distance, he saw a frail old woman. As he approached the old woman, he saw that she was picking up beached starfish and throwing them back into the sea. The young man watched for a while as the woman, again and again, threw starfish from the sand to the water.

Curious, the man asked, "Why are you spending your energy doing what really is a waste of time?" The old woman stopped her throwing for a moment and said, "If these starfish cannot reach the water, they will die." The young man again questioned what the old woman was doing by asking, "There are so very many starfish along this beach. You cannot possibly throw them all back into the water. How are you making any difference?"

The old woman picked up a starfish and held it up to the young jogger's face. Then she tossed the starfish into the sea and said, "It makes a difference to this one."

—Anonymous

Wrapping Our Minds Around The Eternal

We talk of great leaders like Jesus, Gandhi, and Mohammed as if they exist only in the past. When will we learn that we can carry the deceased into the realm of the living? They are still alive ... eternally alive in the hearts and minds of people.

As long as I can picture your face, your face comes to me. As long as I can sing songs we sang together your voice stays in my heart. I have kept you with me despite others saying I need to let go of you and move on. I am going on. People do not understand how you remain alive within me. They cannot see our sacred and eternal bond.

Every major religion of the world has similar ideas of love, the same goal of benefiting humanity through spiritual practice, and the same effect of making their followers into better human beings.

—Dalai Lama

111

Conversations

Talking to a loved one who has died maintains the full circle of life.

> *I stand at your graveside and weep. I talk to you. I feel you hear me. Some say I have gone too far. They say my talking to you as if you were right here only extends my grief. I say these conversations belong to you and me who believe we cannot be separated by time and space. I sense life is far larger than the world in which we live.*

Heaven is the secret we cannot hide and cannot tell, though we desire to do both. We cannot tell it because it is a desire for something that has never actually appeared in our experience ... We cannot hide it because our experience is constantly suggesting it.

—C. S. Lewis in David Van Biema's
Does Heaven Exist?

Seeking Strength In Solitude

Love makes well both the people who give it and the ones who receive it.

> I stand here at your graveside. Our eternal connection draws me to this place. Although I know you have gone on, I find sacred this space where your bones rest. It is a place where I feel the love between us.

The attitude of the Indian toward silence and solitude and secretiveness is distinctive; the stillness within is not something to be dreaded but rather to be sought as a reservoir of spiritual strength.

—Frances Musick in *Pocahontas*

Opening One's Mind To the Universe

They say an empty mind is valuable because it can take in the smells, the sights, and the sounds that surround it. An empty mind absorbs the energy of the trees, the birds, and other animals. A mind too stuffed with information, pride, or vanity is unable to take in the wisdom of the world around it. It cannot hear the leaves sway in the wind, the animals run through the tall grass, or the birds sing. The full mind does not hear.

> *There are days I visit your graveside and I do not know what to say. I just listen. I absorb the energy of the trees, the squawking of the squirrels and the songs of the birds. Having listened, I go back to the world with a calmer mind, taking part of the universe with me.*

One cannot begin to perceive the subtle levels of reality without first quieting the grosser vibrations of the outside world. Everyday reality is so striking that one has to make a conscious effort to downplay it in order to see the other reality that lies behind.

—**Pir Vilayat Inayat Khan** in *Awakening*

114

Wisdom Gained

Many question the existence of a wise and loving God when suffering the loss of someone they love. Why would God create both birth and death?

> Sometimes I think I have learned more about life since your death than I realized in all the years before. Now I understand that experiences with death can change a person. I have learned to love more unconditionally. I have learned to forgive. I now know life is about what you can give to others. I treasure what you gave to me.

Life is willing to teach those who are willing to learn from themselves.

—Vimala Thakar in *The Eloquence of Living*

Time To Think

The habit of silent listening and introspection yields a person who knows the hidden layers of him or herself.

> *I can avoid thinking if I keep busy enough. There are times I purposely surround myself with television, the Internet, and household chores. These distractions leave me little time to think about and connect with what I am feeling. Yet burying my true self for a while provides me no release from your death. I think I had better set aside some silent time with my thoughts of you each day because you are a layer within me.*

It is customary for Vietnamese to eat constantly at memorials for those who have died as well as at celebrations such as the New Year, weddings, and birthdays. Vietnamese eat lots of watermelon seeds. The eating of watermelon seeds has value for three reasons. First, a person can eat a lot of watermelon seeds and not feel stuffed. Secondly, watermelon seeds, even in large quantities, are good for a person's health. The third benefit of eating watermelon seeds is that a person cannot talk while chewing seeds. Not being expected to talk while eating watermelon seeds gives a person more time for reflection, saving words for those times when the person really has something worthwhile to say.

Thich Nhat Hanh in *Fragrant Palm Leaves: Journals 1962-1966*

Honor

A being is created through heredity and nurtured by the environment. Ultimately, each person decides for himself the path he or she will take in life. Everything depends on what a person makes of the gift of genes and place in this world.

> *I go back over the circumstances that led up to your death. But my thoughts are just conjectures when I look at your life from my perspective. Only you know what had meaning for you. Only you could make your decisions. I honor that.*

In this respect, it is important to honor the dead, especially those with whom we've had a close relationship. The soul is not limited in its experience to the confinements of life.

—Thomas Moore in *Soul Mates*

The Meaning Of Your Life

Life has no universal meaning. Its meaning is unique to individuals and their situations.

> *Sometimes I think too much. I try to reason and to figure out just why you died when you did. If I could see you for a little while, there is so much I'd want to ask you. We are inextricably connected in this universe. There has got to be a good reason.*

So many people walk around with a meaningless life. They seem half-asleep, even when they are busy with things that are important. This is because they're chasing the wrong things. The way you get meaning into your life is to devote yourself to loving others, devote yourself to your community around you, and devote yourself to creating something that gives you purpose and meaning.

—Mitch Albom in *Tuesdays with Morrie*

Beyond The Body

Life arises from death.

> *I look at the young people around me and I wonder if they have an inkling of what it is like to lose someone you love. I am changed forever. It is hard to remember the person I was before you died. I have learned that this life has no boundaries. You are with me even though you are not here. With every step I take forward, I now know that life has no end.*

If we are to have clear knowledge of anything, we must be liberated from the body and contemplate things with the soul alone.

—Plato

Invisible Connection

No one is alone. At a deep level, people are joined with a tie that cannot be broken by death.

> *I understand that we are inseparable beings. I can always talk with you. I am open to your spiritual presence. You give shape to the world I live in. I shall never again think I am alone.*

I like thresholds, in-between places, the moments when reality shifts and creaks, when veins of molten eternity gush into the sedimentary layers of time.

—Charles Goodrich in "Remodeling the Hovel,"
The Sun, Issue 320, August 2002

Unconditional Love For Everyone

God loves us unconditionally.

> *I wish to give unconditional love to all the people you loved. That will be my present to you. I try to honor you by doing so.*

We should go with an investigative zeal and with a humble spirit, to learn from the great source of wisdom that is the people.

—**Ernesto 'Che' Guevara in** *The Motorcycle Diaries*

Time With You

Writer Marianne Williamson once said of her friend who died, "Eddie did not die. He is no longer on Channel 4 and our sets are tuned to Channel 4. He is on Channel 7, and he is still broadcasting."

How silly to be boxed in by conventional thought. I'd rather be out there in the world of universal possibility with you. Where you are, there I am also.

Sometimes you need to look reality in the eye and deny it.

—Garrison Keillor

Crying With You

Talking to someone who has died seems a bit far from reality unless we consider that life on earth is only one phase of the reality we all come to know when we pass on.

> *Peace flows from the sky onto me when I stand at your graveside. Here I can say the things I want to say to you that no one else may understand. I can cry with only you watching. This time with you is our time ... our time alone.*

It is such a secret place, the land of tears.

—**Antoine de Saint-Exupéry in** *The Little Prince*

In The Stillness Revering You

Reverence. We honor the dead by remembering them in quiet moments and also at gatherings designed to share memories.

> *I have so many thoughts of you. Some I can share openly. Others never touch my lips. In stillness, I remember.*

Because if you are still, then you will be better able to hear.

—Daniel Quinn in
Ishmael: An Adventure of Mind and Spirit

Setting Aside Differences

At first meeting, most people judge others by clothes, clan, or beauty. To truly know another human being, one must be able to see through these differences to the real person who lies within.

> *I see now your special qualities more clearly. When you were alive, my hopes and fears for you crowded out my sight of the real you. I would say a person can come to know someone better after death. My conversations with you have led me to understand you more dearly.*

Love from one being to another can only be that two solitudes come nearer, recognize and protect and comfort one another.

—Han Suyin

Our Lives Seen In Others

We leave behind the echoes of our lives.

> *I hear evidence of you in the laughter of your child. I glimpse your smile in your brother's face. Your relationship with those left behind shows. You will always be with them and with me.*

The sound stops short, the sense flows on.

—**Chinese Saying**

Graveside

For some who mourn, the graveside provides a place to think in-depth about their loved one. Moonlit nights often provide a background for families praying for the well-being of the one who died.

> *I pace by your graveside and look up. I raise my hands as if to greet you. We touch. Our bond is unbroken by death.*

There is no dark side of the moon ... only a far side.

—Bob McGowan in Martha Gies' *Up All Night*

Connecting With You

We all want our lives to have meaning. We know that it is not so much what happens to us in life that brings this meaning, but rather how our attitude shifts and grows because of the events in our lives.

> *I have made a decision to connect with you every day. One day I may go to the cemetery and place flowers on your grave. Another day I may surprise someone you loved with a note or a gift. Today I may just sit back and, rather than grieve what is lost, be thankful for the unique gift of your life and how your life miraculously intertwined with mine.*

I for one am convinced that if there is such a thing as Heaven, and if Heaven accepts a prayer, it will hide this behind a sequence of natural facts.

—Viktor Frankl

Someone Watching

Sometimes those who grieve feel like their loved one is watching what they do. Those who have lost loved ones often act to make their loved one proud.

> *I used to be able to ignore people and their problems. Since your death, I find myself not turning my back but extending my hand. Your watching me spurs me to lend a helping hand.*

Do every act of your life as if it were your last.

—**Marcus Aurelius**

The Comfort Of Song

Song lyrics often comfort the listener.

> *I'm humming a song we liked and suddenly I find you close to me.*

Sounds like the chant created by a human voice at a Buddhist funeral create a healing frequency.

—Dr. Emoto Masaru in
The Hidden Messages of Water

Past, Present, And Future

Nothing is final. Life is an ongoing stream of events. How you look at life does makes a difference.

You have not been lost, for you are always with me. I carry you with me each day. I live like this is heaven on earth. To me, heaven is a place where spirits gather.

We are always free to choose a different past or a different future.

—**Richard Bach**

All of Us

Many of us get into situations we never intended to get into.

> *Some days I feel like I have stumbled into an unknown land. I did not expect to be dealing with your death. I did not expect to talk to a spirit. Before your death, I would have thought my behavior quite insane. Today talking to you seems akin to beating a drum. I know the sound will be heard out there somewhere.*

The first peace, which is the most important, is that which comes within the souls of people when they realize their relationship, their oneness with the universe and all its power, and when they realize that at the center of the universe dwells the Great Spirit, and that this center is really everywhere, it is within each of us.

—Black Elk in *The Windows of Experience: The Art of Wholeness, Experiential Psychology and the Emergent Self*

Who We Are

Sociologist Margaret Mead said one reason for the generation gap is that grandparents have copped out.

> *I am here for the ones you loved. I can't get enough of people you were close to. Your bond with me reinforces my bond with them. We are all linked.*

... We as social beings through and through, need confirmation by others in order to know who we are.

—Yí-Fu Tuan in *Who Am I?: An Autobiography of Emotion, Mind, and Spirit*

Looking Glass

Robert Frost said, "I always walked my dog. I don't know if it did the dog any good, but it did me."

> *Sometimes I just need to get away from things and walk. I take my thoughts of you along. I walk, speaking to you as if you were beside me. I guess you will always be with me.*

We do not see things as they are.
We see them as we are.

—**The Talmud**

How We Spend Our Time

We all have limitations imposed by time. We need to examine our responsibilities to ourselves and others and decide how we want to spend our limited time.

Looking back to a time before your death, I did not understand regret. Now I do. I would have spent more time with you.

It's not enough to know; you have to begin.

—**Roger Housden** in *Ten Poems to Change Your Life*

Memories Of You

When you are no one, will you be remembered?

> *I cannot hold you close enough. Memories help me.*
> *I am comforted by my thoughts of you.*

Those who survive are consoled by memory alone.

—Jhumpa Lahiri in *The Namesake*

Between The Busyness Of The Day

If we are not careful, we may come to believe our busyness must overshadow times spent in truly meaningful ways.

> *I allow myself time every day to commune with you. Though you are gone, you haunt my mind. And I mean "haunt" in a good way. I like it when good thoughts of you brighten my day. Most times what I am doing is not as important as remembering you.*

Between the idea
And the reality
Between the motion
And the act
Falls the shadow.

—T. S. Eliot

Appreciating Memories

The mystery of life is so evident in nature, in people and in love. When we are in its presence, we know it.

> There are days I look around me and wonder what is real and lasting. It is not what I own but my memories of you that hold the most value for me. My memories are worth more than any of my possessions.

There is a simplicity aesthetic—one aspect of which is appreciation for older things.

The Japanese have a wonderful phrase for this: wabi-sabi, a feeling of appreciation for things whose wear and aging reveal life's impermanence.

—Duane Elgin in *Simplicity and Humanity's Future*

Refocusing My Life

Honoring someone's memory is revering the Great Spirit, who created all.

> *Each step I take is one I wish you to be proud of. My path since your death has veered from an existence about me to a life in which I measure myself by how good, loving, kind, and fair I can be with the people I meet each day. Your death has taught me I may not have tomorrow. I must be who I want to be now, every day.*

The "kingdom of heaven" is a condition of the heart—not something that comes "above the earth" or "after death."

—Fredrich Nietzsche

139

Using Time Wisely

It is written in the Bible that Micah said, "The Lord requires that we do justice, love kindness, and walk humbly with our God."

> *I bow my head at your grave in honor of the mystery that is life. How quickly I have reached my years. Your death has taught me that there is no promise of tomorrow. I must not miss the opportunities of today.*

The utility of living consists not in the length of days but in the use of time; a man may have lived long, and yet lived but a little.

—Michael de Montaigne in Sherwin Nuland's
How We Die

Looking Beyond Everyday Reality

Our world is full of things that on the surface seem unconnected, but actually are. Our view of reality is only a view. It is not reality.

> *Your death has led me to look beyond ordinary reality to the realm of the seemingly unconnected unseen. Like a mirror, your death has given me an otherwise hidden view of myself. For the first time, I see my soul clearly—who I am.*

To be aware of inner harmony is to abide with reality. To abide with reality is to be enlightened.

—Tao Te Ching

Who I Am

Our beliefs about what soul is, who is divine, whether or not an afterlife exists, all affect how we treat other people. What we believe is central to how we form our spirits. You are who you say you are because of what you believe and do, and death will not change your soul.

> *I want to be a good soul. Your death has enhanced my desire to do good in this world and in your name. There are times I want to create something special to capture who you were and what you mean to me.*

I decide on the basis of conscience.

—**Martin Luther King, Jr.**

142

The Invisible World Of You

Our lives are encircled with spirits of another world. We may call on spirits around us for wisdom and strength.

> *I am standing at your graveside. I cry to you out of the depths of my sorrow. I know I must sound mad to others who stand nearby. You are lost to me in this life, but not invisible to me now. And so I speak, like a mumbling fool making sense only to myself and to you. I am not sure my closest friends understand my emotions. But from these grounds that cover your remains, I find strength. And from our talks, I reflect back on life and the loss of you. I sense there must be a reason for all this to have happened this way. I shall trust that God has a plan for me.*

If man does not keep pace with his companions, perhaps it is because he hears a different drummer.
Let him step to the music he hears, however measured or far away.

—Henry David Thoreau

Music Soothes

Music has the ability to change how we feel. Music may instigate changes within us.

> *Often I become lost in thought when I listen to the music you loved. The music transfixes me because it recalls for me your emotions. I feel like I am in a trance from which I do not want to leave.*

*Let us sing a new song
not with our lips
but with our lives.*

—St. Augustine

The Invisible

Death does not erase a relationship. Ancient cultures traveled to burial grounds to commune with people in the otherworld. It is widely believed today that dead spirits come back and contact friends and family. Deceased children visit parents. Living partners reveal that their deceased spouse has appeared before them or talked to them. Many report that someone who has died has reached out and touched them.

> *You visit me. I talk to you. Many people think I have lost it. They do not realize I have found the meaning of our lives. We are pure love for one another. Pure love comes from the creator of all life forms.*

We all have a special faculty to see the invisible and we have to cultivate it.

—Jan Linhorst

Defining Ourselves

It is important to be in touch with our feelings. We own them.

Before your death, I was out of touch with myself. I spent all my time seeking the company of others. I measured myself by the approval of others. Your death has taught me to be conscious of my feelings each moment. I have come to accept myself with my character flaws. I forgive myself for not always being exactly how I would like to be. I find myself laughing when I do things like you used to do. I see that parts of who I am now were formed as imitations of you.

One of the most frustrating things about being middle-aged is that we have to confront the fact that we are who we have been. Those choices we made long ago still define us in many ways, not all of which are ways in which we feel comfortable being defined today.

—Bill Wineke

Living On

The lives of good people reside after death in the hearts and minds of those who loved them. There is an intimacy in this relationship. At times, our memories hurt.

> *You clearly have made yourself present to me, not just as a memory, but in spirit. I have come to know great depths of sadness related to the impermanence of life, and also the great joy the permanence of spirits joined in love brings.*

Only when nobody alive remembers the dead, is death final.

—**Carmen Chavez in** *Celebrate & Live Forever*

Alive In My Heart

Death channels life to us. If we look at our daily life as a source of God's presence, we see how God has extended life beyond the grave. Loved ones who have gone before us still live in our minds and hearts.

> *I think of you daily. There seems to be a channel by which we communicate. You are alive in my heart. Feeling your spirit, I am aware that my time is not really separate from eternity.*

He that wrestles with us strengthens our nerves and sharpens our skills.

—Edmund Burke

Death's Teachings

Death comes always before life.

> *I was the "walking dead" before your death. Life had no real meaning and no good purpose. Your death has heightened my awareness of the goodness of life and how very much I want to be a part of the story that tells that eternity is in our midst, available to us now. I am witness to the fact that death has not taken you away. Death has allowed you to be present with me when I need your strength and support.*

The images are the beginning; you must have the images first. Then comes the road.

—Rainer Maria Rilke

Having You Forever

When you love a person at some time in their life, you have them forever. Life does not go backwards, but good memories do.

> *I loved you before and I love you still. Time spent with you was one of the best parts of my life. Love has joined us forever by what is deepest in ourselves.*

We see what we believe as surely as we believe what we see. All the thoughts we have ever had exist even when we do not think of them, just as rain exists on a cloudy day.

—**Andrea Barrett** in *The Forms of Water*

In the Company Of Those We Love

Two children played in the sand at the beach. They built a castle, complete with a moat that passed from the castle to the water's edge. As the tide came in, a wave made its way up the channel to the castle. Water overflowed the moat. The castle broke down and only a heap of sand stood where the children's masterpiece had been. The children looked at one another and laughed, holding their hands to their mouths until the sand was washed outward to the shoreline. Then they got up and ran further up the shore. There they sat down to gleefully make another sandcastle with a moat. Things don't seem so bad when they're shared.

> *I still hear your voice in my heart. We laughed. We cried. Looking back, it is the feeling of closeness between us I treasure most.*

Traveling in the company of those we love is home in motion.

—Leigh Hunt

How Do You Know?

Psychologist Carl Jung proposed that meaningful coincidences suggest something more is going on in this life than meets the eye. He called these coincidences "synchronicities." Synchronicities make us feel that our connections with people were meant to be, and often happened to teach us something.

> *I grew up knowing the usual limitations of physical space and time. I knew life was time-limited. But this fact never bothered me until you died. Your death has taught me to be open to that realm of experiences that transcends life here on earth. Your death has been a lesson for me in immortality. If not for you, I would only see what meets the eye. Instead, I know that life may connect people in many ways for purposes not evident to us at first. Hindsight often reveals that things were meant to be.*

An old man had a horse. One day, the horse ran away. The neighbors came by to offer sympathy. "That's really bad!" they said. "How do you know?" asked the old man.

The next day the horse returned, bringing with it several wild horses. The old man and his son shut all the horses in a fence. The neighbors said,

"That's really good that the horse came back."
"How do you know?" asked the old man.

The following day, the old man's son tried to ride
one of the wild horses. He fell off and broke his
leg. The neighbors said, "That's really bad." How
do you know?" asked the old man.

The day after that the army came conscripting
local young men into the army to fight in a far-
away war. The old man's son couldn't go to war
because he had a broken leg.

—Paraphrased from a story in Benjamin Hoff's
The Te of Piglet

Transcendence

"Transcendence" comes from the Latin word meaning to "climb over." In practical terms, transcendence describes a state of mind that has progressed from ordinary to one that is beyond the normal, rational mind.

> *Alone, I am swept up in thoughts of you. The people and things around me fade into oblivion. I have transcended this life and have stepped into yours.*

I believe who we are is not what we think we are and what is seeable. Who we are is more than the body or the personality.

—Ram Dass

Our Real Selves

Many people can see the outer path on which people travel in life. Career, family, homes, and cars—these speak of who a person seems to be. Fewer people, however, can see the inner path a person is pursuing. Trust, faithfulness, honesty—these speak of whom a person is inside.

> *People say you died too young. But as I look back, I now can see you developed your real self ... your authentic self. You reached further than most people to become truthful, courageous, accepting, and caring.*

To me people are whole when they have the guts to live out their convictions in their lives, when they can face difficult situations and everyday choices in a way that honors what is inside of them.

—Marsha Sinetar in *Ordinary People as Monks & Mystics: Lifestyles for Self-Discovery*

Perceptions Of Reality

We may never grasp what heaven is really like while we live on earth. This story has been passed on for ages to reinforce what reality really is.

In India, long ago, six blind men came upon an elephant.

"I've walked into a wall," the first blind man said.

"I've found a spear," said the second.

The third blind man, like the others, relying on his sense of touch, exclaimed when feeling the movement of the elephant's trunk, "It is a snake."

"It's a tree," the fourth blind man cried out as he tried to encircle one of the elephant's legs with his arm.

"Oh, what a fine fan," the fifth blind man whispered as he relaxed in the breeze blown over him by the elephant's swaying ear.

The sixth blind man grabbed onto the elephant's tail, and feeling its coarseness declared, "I have found a rope."

Like the blind men, we may not always understand what we feel. It takes time and effort to realize what truly is.

—Anonymous

> *I continue to leave ordinary reality and talk to you. My "chatter" nourishes me. I feel less alone when I communicate with you. I imagine you see me and others whom you left behind. We are here trying to move forward, trying to imagine where you are, and never, for a moment, forgetting our love for you. I cannot know what you now know. I cannot feel how you now feel. I cannot see what you now see. I cannot hear sounds you now hear. But I know you are here with me.*

Though his ashes have been scattered into the Ganges, it is here, in this house and in this town that he will continue to dwell in her mind.

—Jhumpa Lahiri in *The Namesake*

Helping Each Other

Sometimes all it takes for people to share themselves is recognition of the common threads of life. Everyone and everything is related.

> *I met a man who had just lost his mother. I walked up to him and said, "I am sorry for your loss. I know it's hard. I've been through it myself." The man leaned on my shoulder. I then said to him, "Don't give her up. Don't ever give her up. She will always be with you. If you are open to her presence, each day for the rest of your life you will feel her guiding you." The man said nothing and went on his way. I hope I can share what I have learned from your death and help others through their painful times.*

There's an old story that tells of a woman who lived a long and worthy life. When she died, an angel came to her and said, "Come with me and I will show you Hell." The woman was guided to a room full of people sitting in a circle around a huge pot of stew. Each person held a long-handled spoon that reached to the pot but was too long to reach their mouth. Everyone was tired and cranky. Everyone was desperately hungry.

The angel then guided the woman to a place called Heaven. The woman saw a room identical to the first room. A group of people were seated around a big pot of stew. Each person held the same kind of long-handled spoon. But in this room, the people were chatting and happy. Laughter filled the air. "What is going on?" asked the woman. The angel smiled and said, "But don't you see? Here they are using the long-handled spoon to feed each other."

—Paraphrased from a story in John Robbins'
Diet for a New America

Seeking Meaning

When face-to-face with death, we may learn what is important about life. Finding the meaning of life is a spiritual quest.

> *Now I see that life is a lesson of learning to give love and to receive love. I will care for those you dearly loved.*

We seek inner coherence, a narrative thread, something that gives us a sense that our lives matter, that there is meaning to what we do. We know that we will die and we will want to know that there is a purpose to our living.

—Norvene Vest in
Desiring Life: Benedict on Wisdom and the Good Life

Prayer

People often assume they can make spiritual experiences happen by going to the right church or temple, wearing the right bracelet, or saying the right words of prayer. What is spiritual, however, is not necessarily religious, and what is religious is not necessarily spiritual.

> *I go to church and worship. I am comforted by spiritual rituals and messages. Afterward, I walk to your grave. I speak to you not so much to be heard but to better understand myself. It is here I am transformed and made whole again.*

Prayer is the search for God in all things and people.

—Esther de Waal in
Seeking God: The Way of St. Benedict

Sharing Yourself

Life stories are like glaciers. If you look only at what is on the surface you may miss the greater part that lies hidden under the water. We all have a story. Sharing our stories with our loved ones gives roots to generations that follow.

> *You are one of the most important characters in the story of my life. I talk about you a lot. Those who never met you know you through me. To celebrate your life, I share stories about you with your loved ones who did not have enough time with you.*

The human contribution is the essential ingredient. By giving of oneself to others, we truly live.

—Ethel Percy Andrus

Life's True Happiness

In the end, success is not measured by what you accomplished in this lifetime, but rather by how you treated those around you on your journey.

> There were many times you made me proud. We had fun celebrating your successes. But nothing has brought me more happiness than your love for me.

Two elderly men chatted on a bench at an art gallery. Each had been an artist. One man taught art in a high school. The other man was a famous painter whose pictures hung in galleries around the world. Over time, the two men became friends and visited art galleries together. Each time they met, the teacher shared cookies his grandchildren had baked.

One starry evening, as the men sat outside enjoying the sky, the high school teacher said, "I always dreamed of painting a masterpiece like you. I tried to paint that well but I failed."

"You fool," said the artist, "Don't you realize that every man paints only one masterpiece and that is his life; what he does with it and what he lets life do to him. Do my paintings bring me cookies? Right now my paintings are alone in dark museums just like I am."

—Paraphrased from a story told by Richard McLean in
Zen Fables for Today

Embracing Life

Life is difficult. We endure both good and bad experiences that change us. We grow in awareness of who we are and who we want to be. Attentiveness to who we are as a spirit makes sense of all the trials and suffering inherent in life on earth. By looking beyond this life and raising our current consciousness to a higher level, we illuminate the holiness of our personal experiences.

> *I hold you in my awareness forever. As I go about the chores of my life, your luminosity stays with me. Nothing in life can hurt me as much as losing you. I have learned that life on earth is limited, but spirits commune forever.*

We have to be here to learn, otherwise our difficulties are truly meaningless.

—Ram Dass in
Still Here, Embracing Aging, Changing and Dying

Becoming More

We are impermanent. As each day passes, our old self is replaced by our new self. Some people remain stoic— rock-like, unchanged by passing time. Others are sculpted more deeply with each passing experience. Their new selves are formed from their former selves, plus new experiences and thoughts.

> *I can say for myself that your death has changed me. I have learned more about my faults and weaknesses. I have come to be more forgiving of myself and others. I think you would be happy your death has brought about a better, more loving and caring human being.*

A life spent making mistakes is not only more honorable but more useful than a life spent doing nothing.

—**George Bernard Shaw**

Uneven Edges

We all have uneven edges. These uneven edges speak to our lack of wholeness without each other. It is in complementing someone else that we make our beings full. Like cogs in a machine, we intertwine with someone else to fashion one of the many circles of our lives.

> *Your spirit. My spirit. Our circle. Your eyes. Your voice. Your touch. Now that you are gone, my edges unravel and I feel simultaneously awash with uneasiness for not having done more and joy for what we did together. My heart sighs deeply. I cannot put into words the depth of my longing for another chance with you. I know I must be patient. And patient I will be. Our reunion. Our circle. Our uneven edges bandaging each other's uneven edges. God's plan so clear. Wisdom comes when we reflect on our experiences. Hard as life can be, the many circles of intertwining and uneven edges teach us that the purpose of life is to become whole with one another.*

Ours is a time of emerging awareness of the interconnectivity of all things.

Matthew Fox in *The Coming of the Cosmic Christ: The Healing of Mother Earth & the Birth of Global Renaissance*

Chapter Three
Feeling the Stages of Grief

The world doesn't stop because you need some time to grieve.

Elisabeth Kübler-Ross (1926-2004), a pioneer in human response to death and dying, spent time with grieving people. Some were grieving for their own upcoming death. Others were grieving over the loss of loved ones.

In "On Death and Dying," Kübler-Ross identifies stages that people naturally go through as their loss is processed. These stages are known worldwide as denial, anger, bargaining, depression, and acceptance.

Most people who grieve experience these emotions. This book describes those experiencing grief as *mourners.* The feelings that accompany their actual or anticipated loss are referred to as *grief.*

Mourners select their own pathway through grief. There is no right or wrong passageway through the death of a loved one. My experience working with patients facing death and those left behind when loved ones die has shown that *how* and *if* the above emotions are displayed vary from person to person. Mourners may pass through stages of denial, anger, bargaining, depression or loss only to re-experience it again later. Rituals—religious and spiritual—seem to bolster the mourner's equilibrium.

So why doesn't grief precisely follow the stages identified by Kübler-Ross? The answer, simply put, is that every one of us is different. Each of us has had a unique relationship with the person who is dying or has died. We see death through the filter of our experiences with the dying or deceased. We do not all view death the same way because we see death as we are ... through *our own eyes*.

Some mourners prefer to keep their grief hidden. Not everyone is comfortable sharing anger with friends. The mourner may reveal this emotion only to family members. Anger may be placed on someone or something that was not the real cause of the death. Some mourners fall into depression and have a hard time climbing out. They see their future as terminally bleak; they shut down and limit conversation about their feeling of loss. Widows and widowers may have gone through long, drawn-out, and painful illnesses with their spouses. For those who anticipated the death for so long, acceptance may come sooner and they may move on with their lives quickly. This pre-processing of the inevitable death of a loved one is called *anticipatory grief*.

Because many mourners slip and slide back and forth through the recognized stages of grief, one day the person may appear to accept the loss and the next day show signs of depression. Mourners who feel guilt because they believe they could have done something to prevent the death may experience anger with themselves. The mourner's anger may be stirred up when the cause of death on the autopsy form becomes known. Anger may arise when people around the mourner avoid mentioning the name of the loved one lost and/or do not share in talking about good memories with the mourner. The mourner may feel alone in wanting to bring the lost loved one into the conversation.

Grieving cannot be encapsulated in a specified time period. *Bereavement* is defined as the period of time in which mourning takes place. Just as the emotions of grief vary with each mourner, the length of bereavement also differs with each mourner. This makes sense because grief changes those who mourn. Mourners experience shock as they enter the bereavement period. Little do mourners know at the outset that, when all is said and done, they will be forever changed by experiencing the loss of someone they love.

Though society often suggests otherwise, time does not heal all wounds. The mourner is at increased risk for disease and death in the first two years after death of a loved one. Even if the mourner denies their angst and emotions, their unconscious mind sends messages of conflict throughout the body. Tension and inner conflict may not show on the surface. The mourner may keep their feelings under wraps, knowing that baring them for an extended period is frowned upon in today's fast-paced world.

We all want to control our feelings and not be governed by them. Mourners have a way of dealing with the stressful, often-conflicting emotions of grief. They can dispel the notion that grief has an end. Instead, mourners can give themselves permission not to cut the ties with their loved one. This book contains readings that enable the mourner to manage their grief by bringing the deceased into their conversations. The passages are written to help the mourner communicate honestly, both with people in their lives and with the lost loved one. This process is called *remembrance*.

Remembrance, then, becomes another stage of the grief cycle. The process of remembering helps the mourner adapt to death in a healthy, positive, life-affirming way. Communication with and about the deceased allows the mourner to better understand what the lost loved one brought to the mourner's life. Remembrance affirms that the lost loved one continues, in spirit, to affect the heart and soul of the mourner. Just as mourners learn how deeply one human being has affected them, so will those who grieve better understand the significance of their own actions toward others who face loss.

Remembrance raises consciousness and reminds us that the body is impermanent, but that spirits affect each other's hearts and lives forever.

Table 1: Recognizing Stages of Grief

Grief Stages	Example Statement Related to the Grief Stage
Denial	"They cannot be sure it was my son in the accident. I have to go with the officers to look at the body. I will wait until I see."
Anger	"Why me? What have I done to deserve this?"
Bargaining	"I would gladly exchange my life, as old as I am, for hers, which was just beginning."
Depression	"I cry every day. I will not see him drive a car, graduate from school or marry."
Acceptance	"I am okay. I am ready to go on."
Remembrance, the new and natural stage	"One day, when I had other plans, you died. After the numbness and anger wore off, I began to stumble onto lessons. I am healing. I am loving people more. As I move forward, I take you with me."

Denial

Shining Forth

Ancient people believed that when a person died, they took their personality with them to the afterlife. They said that, after death, a person was in a blessed state, which was called a "shining forth."

> *This day you are dust. And I cannot believe it is so. I tell people that you are ashes, but when I hear my own words, I do not believe them. For you can never be mere dust to me. You are more. I feel your love.*

The world is round and the place, which may seem like the end, may also be only the beginning.

—Ivy Baker Priest

Healing Love

Ancients believed the deceased could travel from the other world back into life. Ancients invoked the dead to come back and help them with living.

> *I did not think you would die. I beg you to help me through this grief.*

The only thing I know that truly heals people is unconditional love.

—Elisabeth Kübler-Ross in *The Wheel of Life*

What Grief I Am In

For a long time, people have been told that those who grieve the loss of someone dear clearly pass through stages of shock, denial, and anger before becoming more accepting of the death. People are told to expect to pass through distinct stages as time progresses. But for many who grieve, there is no set pattern for these emotions.

Feelings of shock, anger and denial *slide back and forth across each other.* Sometimes people who are very, very angry act as if they accept what has happened. They often do this to spare the people around them from misery. Perhaps there is no reason other than mankind's invention for slotting grieving into stages.

Such an explanation may stifle true feelings from being recognized and shared by the person with the loss.

It is in sharing our feelings—putting words to them and communicating what we feel—that we come to understand ourselves. Grieving does not end. It lasts a lifetime. Every day people who grieve carry their loss on their backs.

I read books on grieving that talk about the stages a person goes through when a loved one dies.

Shock: When I was told you died, I said, "No that cannot be." There are mornings I awaken and say again, "This cannot be."

Denial: I slip in and out of reality, wishing I would awaken from this nightmare.

Anger: I hold my anger inside. My stomach aches. My head is fuzzy. I cannot think straight. I make many mistakes. I am forgetful.

Acceptance: I am told that time will heal me. I am told my sadness will end. But I carry your death through every moment of every day. Although family and friends think it best for me to get over you, I think it is better for me to remember you.

Benedict's voice remains calm—persevere, bear one another's burdens, be patient with one another's infirmities of body or behavior. And when the "thorns of contention" arise daily in life, daily forgive, and be willing to accept forgiveness.

—Kathleen Norris in *The Cloister Walk*

Tears Of Grief

Grief defines us. The pain takes its toll as death seeps into our bodies and souls.

> *I have no appetite. No sleep. Little humor. I don't even try to be my old self. My old self is gone. In its place is a person loving and missing you.*

Unshed tears leave a deposit on your heart.

—**Susanna Tamaro in** *Follow Your Heart*

The Missing Piece

We are not as separate as we think we are. We are actually connected to each other on many levels. Death of a loved one makes us aware that part of us is missing.

> *I cry so hard. Everyone knows your death has broken me. I sincerely try to pick up the pieces of my life. But you are a big missing piece. I talk aloud to you to let you know that I realize we will meet up again.*

I feel fragmented, broken in pieces like a puzzle all spread out on the table. None of the pieces are together and I am not even sure if they will fit together. There are so many pieces that I fear I will not be able to put them back together. Is it an insurmountable task?

—**Carol Pregent in Joyce Rupp's**
Little Pieces of Light: Darkness and Personal Growth

Repressing My Emotion

For some who grieve, periods of denial provide a respite from facing the death of a loved one.

> *Please don't correct me if I take a break from grieving. It doesn't mean I love you less. You can't take my denial away from me. Denying you are gone is a comfort sometimes.*

Everyone has things they can't fix.

—Ellen Gilchrist in *Sarah Conley*

Hoping Things Will Get Better

They call it the pride of youth—the notion people have that they won't die young. We think dying is for the old. When young people die, friends stop to think for a moment that death can happen to them. We only live for a little while in the scheme of the universe.

> *Some days your life feels like a dream. I want to wake up and find you still here. Feeling sad was not your style, so I try to think things will get better in a little while.*

Now I've learned the hard way that some poems don't rhyme and some stories don't have a clear beginning, middle and end.

—Gilda Radner in *It's Always Something*

Going On

Healing is not the same as curing. Curing would mean we go back to our prior state. Healing is like a balm that enables us to inch forward even though we may hurt.

> *I don't want to go through this grieving. Why me? I want your death to be reversed. People say my grief will end. But I think I will feel only palliative consolation. I always will have the wound of losing you.*

Sometimes we stare so long at a door that is closing that we see too late the one that is open.

—Alexander Graham Bell

Memorable Times

To counteract negative emotions, we must send out emotions of the opposite frequencies. Negative emotion will be cancelled by positive emotion. Where there is hate, show love and thankfulness. Where there is anger, show helpfulness and kindness. When fear strikes, show courage. When you are feeling anxious, picture peace in your mind.

> *I have noticed that when people come up to me with so much sadness that they are unable to say your name, I become more gloomy. When people come up to me and talk about you and memorable good times, I am happy. I am healed by people who recognize that you still exist and that you are an important part of my life. I am able to find you again. These times are beautiful.*

I see her in bits and slices, like light streaming through chinks in bricks, in instances that surprise me as beautiful.

—E. Minot

Being Me

Everybody needs somebody with whom they can be their true self.

> *With most people, I still wear a mask that covers my sadness about your death. Being impenetrable to a real sharing of feelings, my mask filters conversation. Only with my true friends can I be myself and discuss thoughts of you.*

The way you are broken tells me something unique about you. That is the reason for my feeling very privileged when you freely share some of your deep pain with me, and that is why it is an expression of my trust in you when I disclose to you something of my vulnerable side.

—Henri Nouwen

The Imponderable

Learning does not always take place at the moment you would think. Often, we analyze the data and draw our conclusions long after an event.

> *I thought and thought today. I still cannot answer the fundamental question, "Why did you die at this time?" Maybe I will come up with the answer some other day. Maybe your death will always be an imponderable ... something that cannot be explained away.*

When one does not understand death, life can be very confusing.

—**Achaan Chah** in *A Still Forest Pool: The Insight Meditation of Achaan Chah* **edited by Jack Kornfield**

Going On

That the world goes on at its regular pace after a loved one's death often makes those grieving confused. It takes time to process loss. You can't just push someone's life into your subconscious and go back to work as if what has happened is simply a done deal. When we lose someone important to us, we do not go on as usual. We may be in our usual places, but our minds and hearts—torn and battered by loss—are fragmented and often not able to keep up with the pace others around us expect of us.

> *I am with you one way or the other. I bring you to work with me. I bring you driving in my car. Perhaps, over time, you will fade into the background fabric of my life. Right now, I still cannot live this life without your presence on the surface of each day.*

I am as frightened as you are.

—**Rosina Lippi in** *Homestead*

Helping Someone Helps You

Holiness can be found in daily acts of kindness and generosity. A woman baking bread for her family. A man sharing tools with a neighbor. People helping people. Daily life is full of sacred moments. All we have to do is recognize and mimic them.

> *Friends brought me meals. Family held me tightly. These little things meant a whole lot to me. It is as if there were sanctity around your death, a sacred time when all who were with me sought ways to help me out. I will try to give to others the same that was given to me when their time comes to grieve.*

Dr. Karl Menninger, a renowned psychiatrist, once gave a lecture on mental health and was answering questions from the audience.

"What would you advise a person to do," asked one man, "if that person felt a nervous breakdown coming on?"

Most people expected Dr. Menninger to reply, "Consult a psychiatrist." To their astonishment, he replied, "Lock up your house, go across the railway tracks, find someone in need and do something to help that person."

Always Seeing You

There is no way out of what life hands us. We must experience it all. We cannot turn back the pages of our life. We must go forward, trusting in ourselves, in mankind, and in circumstances. Our strength is tested when we experience the death of a loved one.

> *Your death is inescapable. It haunts my days. It comes to me in dreams. I would like to live again in the time before you died. Days without you are difficult. The only way through these sad days is to cherish the life we shared. And I do.*

My tears have dried from their place of rest. I see her with the eye in the back of my head.

—**Anna Ruth Henriques** in *The Book of Mechtilde*

My Voice

Thinking should precede talking. Silence should be a time in which to arrange our thoughts before we speak.

> *I hear people talk about you. And I can say nothing. Thoughts of you overwhelm me. I am still trying to make sense of your death. There is too much I do not understand. I need time to think alone before I will speak.*

We must be quiet, even silent, to begin to deeply empathize with others.

—**Stephen R. Covey in**
The 8th Habit: From Effectiveness to Greatness

Echoes Of Friendship

Traditions pull out words from the depths of our hearts to explain our feelings.

> *Every time I stand by your grave, I ask, "Why? Why now? Why were you taken from me?" I know that into every life some tragedy must fall. I am trying to absorb my share. I am not healed. I do not know if I ever will be. I go on a changed person, trying to exist with echoes of you inside me.*

What is a friend?
A single soul dwelling in two bodies.

—Aristotle

Behaviors Come From Emotion

It is a basic human survival response to put distance between ourselves and situations that hurt us. We don't touch a hot stove. We test bath water before stepping in. We leave alone electrical wires downed by storms. Some people also remove objects that remind them of painful experiences. A newly divorced man may purchase a new car his ex-wife has never driven. A victim of a motorcycle accident may sell his bike. Keeping mementos of someone whom we loved but lost to death is an exception to this distancing of things that hurt and may remind us of the past. A grieving person does not need to remove all reminders of a lost loved one. A parent who lost a child or a child who has lost a parent may find comfort in seeing a picture of the loved one. The deceased's photo albums, favorite music, and books may console the family that lives on and provide avenues of connection with the deceased.

> *Your brother told me the other day that seeing me reminds him of your death. And so to relieve himself of discomfort, he comes by less frequently. He tells me he is busy with this and that. I know these are just excuses designed to put distance between him and his loss. Since your death, he has built a new life. Whereas I need to have pictures of the past around to console me, he wants none. Maybe the sorrow of your death has hurt him so much that he cannot connect with you or me right now. I pray he will heal enough to reach outside himself and feel your touch and mine.*

What he may not dare to think, he often utters in deeds. The heart is revealed in deeds.

—Abraham Heschel in *Seeds of the Spirit: Wisdom of the Twentieth Century,* edited by Richard Bell & Barbara L. Battin

Living

The promise of meaning enables us to survive. Yet we must live in today.

> *Until this year, I felt like I was living quite an ordinary life. Your death has changed that for me. Death no longer feels like a statistic. It is something I must live with each day.*

It is not death that a man should fear, but he should fear never beginning to live.

—Marcus Aurelius

Anger

It Hurts So Much ... I Am Angry

It is not what happens to you in life that reveals most about you. It is what you do with what happens that is significant. For some people, life is an interesting challenge. For others, it is one crisis arriving on the heels of another. Our personal perspective and philosophy of life underlies what we accept, what we fight for, and who and what we love.

> *I am spending a lot of time persuading myself not always to be angry about your death. Anger is tiring and brings me little solace. Looking at your death as just one phase of your life comforts me.*

Anger is a great obstacle. The after-effects of anger are frustration and depression. If we allow anger, the thief, to enter into us, then it will steal our love, which is our inner treasure. When anger assails us, we must cry inwardly for deep inspiration to come to the fore and chase it away.

—**Sri Chinmoy** in *The Wings of Joy*

Thoughts

Thoughts have energy. We can express thoughts or keep them to ourselves. Some believe that if you hold good thoughts, good will come to you. Others believe that if you do not express negative thoughts, the energy in the thoughts can harm you.

> _When you died, I was mad. I still feel some measure of anger at the circumstances of your death. I try to control my angry feelings and replace them with appreciation for the time we had. This is hard to do. It seems so natural to fall into a state of disillusionment. What pulls me out is knowing that you would want me to hold good thoughts of you._

Human beings are not always aware of what they are feeling. Like animals, they may not be able to put their feelings into words. This does not mean they have no feelings.

—Jeffrey M. Masson & Susan McCarthy in _When Elephants Weep: The Emotional Lives of Animals_

Our Choice

Life calls us to be more tomorrow than we are today. We have a choice to respond to our circumstances with a positive or a negative attitude. We can build on our past rather than let our past harm our future.

> *I feel kind of growly. I grumble more lately. I am having a difficult time pretending I'm all right. I want to get beyond this time of grief. I want to be happy again. Please help me.*

She had no idea where she wanted to go, only that she had to get away from the place where she'd come up against her own brokenness.

—**Ursula Hegi** in *Stones from the River*

Beating Feeling Hurt

People who grieve find themselves keeping their anger in check most of the time. They keep the lid on. It is not unusual, however, that those who grieve unintentionally displace their anger onto the people who happen to be next to them. Elisabeth Kübler-Ross, physician and death counselor, often gave people who were grieving a piece of rubber garden hose with the instruction to, when angry, beat it on a bed, pillow, or floor.

> *Someone gave me eighteen inches of rubber tubing. I don't know what to think. Maybe I will do as she suggests and beat the wall with it. Or slam the rubber tubing on my car's hood. I am so mad you died. I guess it is worth a try.*

Actually, the bitterest people are those who have the least faith in their own capacity to heal, to change, and to grow. Bitterness arises from the realization that the world has defeated one's hopes or expectations, but bitterness thrives on the belief that no comfort or solution for one's original hurt can ever be found.

—D. Patrick Miller in *The Book of Practical Faith: A Path to Useful Spirituality*

Picturing You

When people we love die, we often define the stages of our lives in terms of the time before their deaths. We have all heard people say things such as, "When your mother was alive," and "When grandpa was here to tell the story," and so forth.

> *My life now has been divided into two parts: the life*
> *I had with you before your death and the*
> *relationship I have with you now, after your death. I*
> *choose to carry you with me. I will never leave you*
> *in the past.*

The way you changed my life. No, no they can't take that away from me.

—George Gershwin and Ira Gershwin in
"They Can't Take That Away From Me"

That Which Endures

No one is excluded from the role of heavenly messenger. It is our job to listen for the messages of the people in our lives.

> *I rage against your death. I scream in anguish. And afterwards, I pray that I may understand why life has turned out this way.*

Behold this one flaming truth: All life is fleeting. Cling to that understanding and seek then, within yourself, that which alone endures.

—Omar Khayyam

Angry

We can know intellectually that every "good-bye" at death is accompanied by a "hello" in an unseen world. Knowing this does not change our longing to reconnect with our loved one who has died.

> *Who picked the time you would die? What is this master plan? I am angry. I am sad. I can think of no good reason why you died.*

The God that comes before skepticism may bear little resemblance to the God that comes after.

—**M. Scott Peck** in *The Road Less Traveled*

Making Up For Imperfection

The Rule of Benedict teaches that if I have a dispute with someone, I should make peace before the sun goes down.

> *I remember my mama saying that we children should make up before we went to sleep. Sometimes we did. Other times we did not. There are hurt feelings among our family. And now there is no way back. I cannot change my past inertia. My heart aches. Demons haunt me, saying, "Why did you not forgive more?"*

A perfect person would be inhuman. I like the fact that in Chinese art the great painters included a deliberate flaw in their work: human creation is never perfect.

—**Madeleine L'Engle in** *A Circle of Quiet*

Ignoring Reality

So much of social life is exhausting. We pretend to be okay so we do not hurt another's feelings. We do not want to be a burden to others.

> *I feel so many outside pressures to conform and end my grieving. Sorry, but my grief will not stop. I limit my friendships to those who understand that I continue to spend some time in nostalgia, remembering you. I have let acquaintances who resist my talking about you drift away. Your name is on my lips and I must speak it.*

They never discussed what they used to do; they never spent time alone together. Win was wrapped up in a web of lies about as dense as hers, and when he looked at her now, his eyes shot off to the sides.

—**Andrea Barrett** in *The Forms of Water*

Channeled Through Ordinary People

The love of God comes to us through people. Ordinary people can heal others.

> *These days are tough. My anger spews out at home and at work for no discernible reason. I ask your presence in my life to help me balance my emotions as I wade through my grief.*

Of course there are moments when I do get angry but in the depth of my heart, I do not hold a grudge against anyone.

—Dalai Lama

201

Allowing Grieving

In our culture, there is little time for grief. We are expected to be stoic and resume our lives quickly when someone we love dies. It is important to allow ourselves to grieve.

> *I am not overly melancholy, but every day I look inward and think of you. I am astounded how little I am asked about how I am doing, how I am grieving. People act like nothing happened to me. But I have been changed in a most profound way. I want to say to people, "Talk with me about my loss."*

It takes a friend to want to hear your story, no matter where it goes.

— **Anne Raver** in *Deep in the Green*

Still Mourning You

Death inflicts a wound that may deepen each day. Suffering and loss may become ingrained in the fiber of the person who grieves. This spiritual pain may not be obvious to others because the person may cover their loss with a cheerful demeanor.

> *When I'm at work feeling sad for the loss of you,*
> *people with whom I share my day are too busy, too*
> *distracted or unfeeling to even comment on my pain.*
> *I feel indisposed and invisible. People stare right*
> *through me. I think my sorrow shows, but no one*
> *connects with my soul. Society expects me to be*
> *done with my grieving. No one sees me still*
> *mourning the loss of you.*

No matter how much you may have read about
the experiences of others, you can't ever be
prepared for the intense feelings that will engulf
you when you have suffered a great personal
loss.

—Helen Fitzgerald in *The Mourning Handbook*

Transcending The Body

Wise men see beyond the form in which the body exists to the non-worldly essence that transcends the body.

> *I am tired of people saying you are gone. Why do they not know you are still with me? I guess some people only say they believe in life after death. They act like life beyond death is not real.*

The body is only a garment. How many times you have changed your clothing in this life, yet because of this you would not say that you have changed. Similarly, when you give up this bodily dress at death, you do not change. You are just the same, an immortalized soul, a child of God.

—Parmahansa Yoganada

Sit by Me, My Friend

Every word is like a seed, planting an idea, a feeling, an inspiration. Words are powerful. Too often today, people talk without thinking. Their silence would speak volumes more than their words.

> *So many people talk at me, trying to distract me from the loss of you. I am having a hard time responding to all their chatter. I want to say, "Go away unless you have something really important to share." Idle chatter to me is just noise. I wish just one person would take my hand and sit with me in silence. Being with me in silence would be more comforting.*

Friend: one who knows all about you and loves you just the same.

—**Elbert Hubbard in David McNally's**
Even Eagles Need a Push

Mirror, Mirror Who Am I?

Mostly we are uneven people. We have our slick and smooth sides—the masks we show others. But we also have our cuts, bruises and crevices—our worn spots, the places where we have experienced loss.

> Today I was mad at people I love. I didn't mean to be. Today I just couldn't pretend I wasn't sad about your death. The days when I am mad are fewer and farther between now but still are like cracks in the surface of my personality. I will try to be more even-tempered, because I know you would want me to be so with those you loved.

Pay the most attention to the opinion of the person in the mirror.

—Jacquelyn Mitchard in *The Rest of Us*

Sit With Me

The God of all healing and grace is with family and friends who have lost those they love dearly.

> There are days I hurt so much I cannot believe there is a master plan divined by God. No god would cut out the very heart of me. But it feels like my insides have abandoned me for some other place. I have no heart. No soul is within me. I cry out to God for help and comfort. I cry out. Is someone listening?

We want people to feel with us more than to act for us.

—George Eliot

Those Who Understand The Change In Me

People who speak the same language tend to find each other.

> I keep my distance from those who think your death was an event of the past. They are like the wind. I hear them but I see through them. Instead, I share my feelings only with those who have shown a spark of understanding about the depth of my loss.

Beyond right and wrong there is a field. I will meet you there.

—Rumi

The Language Of Tears

Everyone needs to cry out at times to express emotions often kept too tightly bound inside our hearts.

> *I find myself in tears for no reason at all. Sometimes it is when I just thought of you. Other times the tears flow and I do not know why. I guess grief finds its expression any time it wants.*

You may find yourself dissolved in tears for no reason at all. An old grief that wasn't allowed expression at the proper time is at last being felt.

—Jill Aigner, OSB, in *Foundations Last Forever: Lectio divina, a mode of scripture prayer*

My Changing Perspective

True happiness comes from seeing life as it is, with all its ups and downs, instead of as we ideally want it to be.

> It took me a long time to understand that not only must I go on without you, but also that life will go better if I give up any anger or bitterness that holds my spirit from communicating lovingly with others.

There are very few human beings who receive the truth, complete and staggering, by instant illumination. Most of them acquire it fragment by fragment.

—Bobby Wolff

Making A Rainbow After The Rain

It is something to be able to paint a picture, or to carve a statue, and so to make a few objects beautiful. But it is far more glorious to carve and paint the atmosphere in which we work, to affect the quality of the day. This is the highest of the arts.

—Henry David Thoreau

> _I could be angry all the time. Maybe I deserve to be. I could be sad all the time. If I dwelled only on loss, not gain or happiness, sadness would shroud my being. I could pretend you did not die and not talk to you or to anyone about you. I could indulge in self-pity that might push those who care about me away. I choose to gather up all the stories we share and weave a rainbow._

Our life is a weaving. We can choose to make it full of color like a rainbow.

—Molly Susanne Boykoff

Out Of Anger

Inner peace makes you peaceful on the outside.

> *I was angry that you died. I denied the facts. I tried to put your death out of my mind. Only later, when I gave myself permission to walk and talk with you in the spirit world, did I find peace.*

Within our darkest moments, our brightest treasures can be found.

—**Marc Allen** in *Tantra for the West*

Bargaining

That's Okay

Buddha found enlightenment when he stopped seeking it and let it come to him.

> *I repeat again and again to myself the circumstances of your death. Was there something I should have done that I missed doing? My friend says that in the end all shall be revealed to me. I wait. I hope.*

True enlightenment and wholeness arise when we are without anxiety about nonperfection. The body is not perfect, the mind is not perfect, our feelings and relationships will certainly not be perfect. Yet to be without anxiety about nonperfection, to understand, as Elisabeth Kübler-Ross, puts it, "I'm not okay. You're not okay. And that's okay," brings wholeness and true joy...

—Third Zen Patriarch in Jack Kornfield's
A Path with Heart

Do

Many regret things left unsaid and undone. If you knew you had only one more day to live with a person, what would you do?

> *Some days I plead with God for some more time with you. I beg. I ask to trade my life for yours. Of course, I know these maneuvers are futile. I would give most anything to have one more day with you.*

Life is not measured by the number of breaths we take but by the moments that take our breath away.

—George Carlin

Meeting Others Who Grieve

We find other people often through coincidence. Our job is to recognize these moments of grace and act, before it is too late, to bring these people close to us.

> *I met a man who also lost a son. He commented that we were lucky to have had sons. He said that his brother was not able to have children. I thought that this was kind of twisted. Then the man added, "You pray for children. You are lucky to have them even for a little while."*

Our faith does not cause us to see different things, but to see things differently.

—Wilkie Au, S.J. in *By Way of the Heart*

Depression

Hearing Myself Think

In today's hectic world, it is often hard to slow our pace and create time to think. People must disengage themselves from the cacophony of television, internet, cell phones, and phone messaging to hear their voice within.

> *People say I am spending too much time alone in thought. They call it brooding. They instead want to crowd my day with movies, get-togethers, and dinners. They tell me I should not think of you so much. They say I will only hurt more. They do not understand that in my quiet times, I leave my hurt behind and enter a place where I can talk to you. Being with you this way comforts me.*

All of us are doing the same thing all the time anyway, all probing the same mystery, asking the same questions. Who am I? Where did I come from? What am I doing here? Is this right?

—Ellen Gilchrist in *Falling Though Space*

Becoming

Everyone has a little voice within. Once in a while we do not listen to that voice and, consequently, we behave badly. It is important to remember that when we fall down on being who we want to be we have the opportunity to pull ourselves up again.

I was not myself today. I just couldn't pull it together. Everyone and everything were bothersome. When the sun rises, I shall climb out of this despair and try again to be the person you knew me as. I want to be that person for you.

The spirit knows that its growth is the real aim of existence.

—Saul Bellow

Being Kind

It has been said that a person never understands the depth of love until the hour of separation.

> *I am continually reminded how much your death has affected me. Grief is nothing I could have ever imagined. I did not know that hurt could be so deep and ever-present. I had no understanding that I would ever feel such an abiding loss.*

Be kind, for everyone you meet is fighting a hard battle.

—**Plato**

You Are A Part Of Me Still

Although we want to be in control of our lives, we are not. Circumstances form and reform us into the person we are.

> *There are days when I cannot look anyone in the eye. I would cry. They do not know how deeply my heart aches for you. They cannot grasp how your death has changed me. I think more. I cry more. I am alone more. Yet I am never without you.*

I am a part of all that I have met.

—Tennyson in *Ulysses*

Peace Within

Enlightenment happens regardless of religion. It happens to all who gain personal insight through the suffering and the small deaths they experience while they are alive.

> *Some days I do not know if I can make it through the day. My sadness drags me down. Other days I realize your death has taught me how to better live each day of my life.*

Only when peace lives within us, will it live outside of us.

—Deng Ming Dao

Death Affects Us

The first year after the death of a loved one a person is more likely to develop first-time cancer, heart disease, and/or depression.

> *I was slumped over and walking slowly, feeling low, talking less. Thankfully, people noticed this change in me. I listened when friends said I was not acting myself, and sought help.*

But over a period of faithful listening, we can expect to discern new patterns woven into our life.

—Jill Aigner, OSB, in *Foundations Last Forever: Lectio Divina: A Mode of Scripture Prayer*

Allowing Grieving

There is no set timetable for mourning. People who grieve may show more sorrow some days than others. Friends and family may need to back off and allow mourners time to grieve.

> I am truthful when I say to my friends that I am not yet able to go out and party. I am not ready. I feel okay in saying "no" for now.

"Yes" can be good. But "no" also can be good.

—Thomas Hora, M.D., metapsychiatrist, in *Beyond the Dream: Awakening to Reality*

Within

Death scratches a scar on the spirit.

> *You are forever engrained in my psyche and in my heart. People say I wear my grief on my sleeve. I know some days I cannot hide my feelings. I am sad and it shows. And it hurts when everyone is going about their day and I am alone in these thoughts of you.*

There is a place in the soul that neither space nor time nor flesh can touch. This is the eternal place within us.

—**Meister Eckhart**

Talk Of Understanding

Sometimes all it takes to understand another human being is listening … putting away the "I" and focusing on the "you."

> *People say, "Move on. It is time." I say, "I cannot imagine life without you." People who have not experienced the depth of loss I have cannot understand me. I am lonely for someone who understands me and will talk with me about my grief.*

So, he came and he sat down right here on the chair next to my bed. I must say, that was nice of him. None of the other doctors sit down. If a person sits down, it's like you're having a conversation. When they stand over you, they're way up there, and you always feel they can't wait to go.

—Betty Rollin in *Last Wish*

Moving Forward

To heal one's own wounds you need to skip the superficial conversations and get down to discussing the pain and suffering inherent in the human condition.

> _I find my best days come after my worst days. It is difficult to talk about you and our relationship. Sharing rubs me raw. But after offering to someone else my vulnerable self, I find myself better able to move forward._

Two monks on a pilgrimage came to a river swollen by recent rains. By the river's bank was a girl obviously wondering how she would get across while not ruining her fancy clothes. One of the monks said to the girl, "Get up on my back. I will carry you. Your dress will not be ruined." The girl took the kind monk's offer and the two crossed the river. The monk put the girl down.

The monks continued walking for an hour or so. Then the monk who did not carry the girl asked, "How could you touch that girl? It is against our order to touch a girl. You broke a rule."

The monk who had carried the girl walked along silently for a while. Then he said, "I set the girl down at the side of the river an hour ago. Why are you still carrying her?"

—Paraphrased from Irmgard Schloegl's
The Wisdom of Zen Masters

227

Our Significance

Death makes us feel vulnerable and insignificant. It forces us to see who we are within the stream of things happening in the world.

> *I cry unto you. Your death has equalized life's playing field. I know now I am no different from the man or woman I pass on the street. I try to hide my grief and walk by. People avert their eyes, pretending they do not see the tears in mine.*

Tailgating thunderclaps rattled the windows, the lamp-black sky spat like a Gatling gun, and lightning bleached the hard-white moon. The massiveness of the drama thrilled me, gave me a proportion, showed me my real size in the scale of things.

—Nick Bantock in *The Forgetting Room*

Acceptance

Blink

When the petals of our lives fall apart, we can look within and, like the rose, be open to the beauty inside.

> *Losing you is the hardest thing that has happened to me. At first, I could not believe you were gone. I was angry and very sad. I tried to bargain with God for your return. My life fell apart. Then I looked within. I found my beautiful memories of you. I felt our bond was not broken. You gave me messages you were all right. Within me a voice said, "Be grateful for the love you have known. Love never dies."*

You can blink and miss it. But you can't make it go away. Your mama's inside of you. You can feel her moving and breathing and sometimes you can hear her talking to you, saying the same things over and over, like watch out now, be careful, be good, now don't get yourself hurt.

—**Carol Shields** in *The Stone Diaries*

Getting Messages

Rituals re-establish our equilibrium. Spiritual practices stabilize and strengthen us in times of stress and confusion. Faith is a positive force that gives us energy to go on.

> *More and more now, I seek out a sanctuary where I can just sit alone. I think. I pray. I allow images of you to come and go. And when I am done, I feel more hopeful than I did before. I am energized by this ritual. Your death has tested my faith.*

Ideal and dearly beloved voices of those
Who are dead, or of those who are lost to us like the dead.

Sometimes they speak to us in our dreams.
Sometimes in thought the mind hears them.

And for a moment with their echo other echoes
return from the first poetry of our lives—like the music that extinguishes the far-off night.

—Greek Poet Cavafy

Writing Down Our Thoughts

Writing our thoughts down on paper helps us understand more clearly how we feel. Journaling, the process of writing about our experiences and feelings, can influence who we become.

> When I look over my life, I wonder, "Was I an important character in your story?" I draw a timeline and write down memorable experiences we shared along the way. Your life has become part of my story. It has changed the way I look at all my life that has followed.

She had so mastered the strategies of camouflage that her own history had seemed a series of well-placed mirrors that kept her hidden from herself.

—Pat Conroy in *Beach Music*

Broken But Stronger

Viktor Frankl, a Vienna psychiatrist and survivor of World War II concentration camps, said that every person has an innate desire to give as much meaning as possible to their life.

Mankind can find meaning not only when performing or creating a work, but also when simply being. Frankl emphasized that mankind can find meaning even in suffering.

> *Some days it seems there are too many things to think about. How can I find a door and let myself out of this suffering? The key seems to be to find meaning in my life and in your death.*

We are what we make, and the moment we stop soul-making we are less than we could be.

—**Robert Sardello in**
Love and the Soul: Creating a Future for Earth

Hope

You need to have patience to have hope. You cannot give up. You cannot give in. You cannot falter from your vision of that for which you hope.

> *My hope for reunion with you keeps me sane. I know we are not as far apart as it may seem today. I trust that our destiny is to be reunited.*

Through hope, we expand the boundaries of what is possible in life.

—**Kathleen Fischer in**
Winter Graces: Spirituality and Aging

Carving Out Good Memory

Learning to see life as it is takes perspective. It is far easier to lose ourselves in ruminating over how life has cheated us.

> *I know that I could be sad all day, all week, all month and all year. I know you would not want me to be so. I know you would want me to pull myself out of my doldrums and enjoy life. I am on the cusp of happiness. I shall not fall off, because I know you wish me happiness.*

The heart's memory eliminates the bad and magnifies the good, and thanks to this artifice, we manage to endure the burdens of the past.

—**Gabriel Garcia Marquez**

Marking Time

Death changes everything.

> *I mark time by when you died. There is the "before," when I lived without fear as if this time on earth would never end. There is the "now," when I live with more respect for the limited time we have on earth.*

But what is in the past remains unchanged, doesn't it? I think it does change. The present changes the past.

—**Kiran Desai** in *The Inheritance of Loss*

Listening And Growing

Stability is defined as the willingness to listen more and stay in a situation in order to grow.

> *I cannot put thoughts of you aside. I will not leave you behind. By carrying you with me every day, I have learned some painful truths. Now I'm a better judge of friends and friendship. I'm a better lover of life and people.*

Listening has something to do with being willing to change ourselves and change our world.

—Joan Chittister, OSB, in
Wisdom Distilled from the Daily

Dust To Dust

As one dies, so dies the other. They all have the same breath, and man has no advantage over the beasts ... all are from the dust, and all turn to dust again.

—Ecclesiastics 3: 19-20.

Sometimes I think you understood what it is that has taken me so long to comprehend. You knew that implicit in each day was an opportunity to take the dust of life and transform it into good experiences. You recognized that this life would end in dust. And in dust it has.

The soil is the great connector of our lives, the source and destination of all.

—Wendell Berry in *The Unsettling of America*

Going With The Flow

Travelers learn this mantra to find their way: Go with the flow. The statement means that when lost in the woods, find a river and follow it to its source. Towns are built near rivers, so following the flow will lead the lost traveler to the safety of a community.

> *Right after your death, there was a constant flow of people and activity. Neighbors came with their casseroles and cakes, and friends arrived to pay their respects. Your memorial service and funeral seemed like surreal events, slowly drawing near and quickly parting. When the burial took place and your headstone was finally laid in place, I shut myself up with my own thoughts. I turned inward and was mostly quiet. I needed this flow of the rituals of death to carry me to a point of reflection. To be with the people who showed me they cared. To talk to friends who listened without judging. To eat among people who cared. This course of events gave my heart and body the nourishment it needed.*

Every bend in the road brings me new ideas and every dawn gives me fresh feelings.

—Benjamin Hoff in *The Te of Piglet*

The Gift Of Listening

Sometimes a listening person, just being a good presence, is all a person who grieves needs.

> *I began to talk about you today, but the person I was talking to was in a hurry to walk away. I wanted some company, but I could not find it. There are days like this. And then there are other days when people notice my grief and listen. For this I am thankful.*

It's scary to think that nobody can see you.

—**Mia Farrow** in *What Falls Away: A Memoir*

The Gift Of Silence

Being truly present for a person is a gift of great magnitude.

> Today my friend said, "How are you?" The friend paused and waited for me to respond. My friend did not hurry to fill the silence. My friend waited for me to put my feelings into words. How compassionate this conversation felt.

It speaks in silence, not words.

—David Steindl-Rast & Sharon Lebell in
Music of Silence: A Journey Through the Hours of the Day

Attitude

Attitude can get in the way of wisdom and happiness.

> *I try to frame my loss of you as one of those things in life I must accept. I try to frame my loss of you as one of those things from which I have learned. Acceptance and learning … these are lofty goals. Many times I can intellectualize them while at the same time I smash them to the floor in a heap like unwashed clothes. I have an attitude about your death, but it is not the same attitude each day.*

One child plays with his balloon until it catches on a branch or a thorn and bursts, leaving him in tears. Another child, smarter than the first, knows that his balloon can burst easily and is not upset when it does.

—Achaan Chah in *A Still Forest Pool: The Insight Meditation of Achaan Chah* edited by Jack Kornfield

Running Toward, Not Away

There was a woman who saw her shadow and was afraid. She decided to run to escape it. As she ran, she turned and looked back. Her shadow was still there. The woman ran faster. Over her shoulder she could see her shadow still following her. Thinking she could outrun what was following her, she ran and ran until she died of exhaustion.

When you first died, gloom and doom followed me each day. I kept trying to get away from the sadness that made me so tired. Then one day I stopped and embraced my sadness. I acknowledged it was real. I decided I could live with it. No longer having to run away from my sadness, I have found more energy to discover how to connect with you where you are now. I am glad I did not let sadness consume me.

How do we know that to cling to life is not an error? Perhaps our fear of its end approaching is like forgetting our way and not knowing how to return home.

—Chuang-tse in *The Te of Piglet*

The Value Of Traditions

Traditions connect generations. Religions comfort people because they represent spiritual truths passed down through the ages.

> *Today is the day of the week I go to church, where I can sing and hold hands with others who believe in the afterlife. In church no one questions me when I talk about your existence on a spiritual plane. My faith is a voice of truth that comforts me.*

The world must have a God, but our concept of God must be extended as the dimensions of our world are extended.

—Pierre Teilhard de Chardin in Ursula King's
Spirit of Fire: The Life and Vision of Teilhard de Chardin

Together

Many times siblings lose contact with one another as they pursue their own dreams. Brothers and sisters find each other at opposite ends of the world and, often, with new and different values. It may take the loss of a parent to bring them together again to see what they have in common.

> *You were one of our branches, but you became untethered. We lost you. Now we hold each other closely and tightly in a shared way of life only those who have lost a loved one can understand.*

Every person needs to resolve the issue of getting ahead versus getting along.

—**Kenneth Pelletier, M.D.** in *Sound Mind, Sound Body*

Lingering Scent

Scent lingers. People who grieve often embrace and smell the clothing and possessions of a lost loved one, thus remembering them in a way more poignant than words could convey.

> *Today I gave away a few more of your things. It's hard. I long to keep them all.*

> *When we smell another's body, it is that body itself that we are breathing in through our mouth and nose, that we possess instantly, as it were in its most secret substance, its very nature. Once inhaled, the smell is the fusion of the other's body and my own.*

> **—Sartre in Annick Le Guerer's**
> *Scent: The Mysterious Essential Powers of Smell*

Taking Time For Each Other

We are rushing en masse to the future, blindly over-looking the moments of today.

> *Today one person took time to ask me how I felt. It's been a while since you died but I still appreciate greatly those who care to stop keeping pace with the world, and instead take the time to shed a caring beam of light on me.*

What would our daily interactions be like if we were not generous with and curious about each other but also willing to make the world a smaller place?

—Kathleen Holt

Chapter Four
Anticipatory Grief

Although it is perfectly natural to do so, we feel uneasy when we find ourselves grieving even before our loved one dies.

For those who have watched a loved one's failing health, grief may start before the person has died. This is a normal reaction to knowing someone is dying. Do not chide yourself for getting your defenses up. It is natural that when we feel a loss coming on, we psychologically prepare ahead so we do not get a "grand slam" when the death happens. Sometimes people feel awkward because they, who sat bedside through the ins and outs of the death, are feeling relief that the ups and downs are over and the loved one no longer is in pain. Those people who have been part of a bedside vigil no longer deny the inevitable.

In contrast, those who are just starting to grieve may question the motives behind such a readiness to move forward. Unlike loved ones who have been at the bedside watching the decline and the effortless slide into the eternal, those whose grief is fresh are going through denial, anger and bargaining, and may not understand that anticipatory grief is normal and okay.

Understanding that some people grieve as their loved one is dying leads us to an important realization. It is okay that loved ones and friends may not be in sync as they slip and slide through the phases of grief again and again until arriving at the place where remembrance overtakes sadness and loss.

Those people closest to the person dying may be ready to face sooner than others the truth that the lifeless body in bed is not the real person. The body, no longer needed, has been abandoned. The real person is a spirit.

Dying Acts

Families ask nurses, "What is on my loved one's mind while wasting away a little more each day?"

> *I am having a hard time watching your suffering. I see your physical wasting as a sign that you are leaving me. I must let go of you. I hear you talk to people I cannot see. You talk about leaving this place to go to another world.*

The person may speak to or see people who are not there, often those who have died before.

—Denise Glavan, Cindy Longanacre & John Spivey in
Hospice: A Labor of Love

Final Acts

Those who are freshly grieving may harshly criticize those who no longer are tearful because they have been at the loved one's bedside day in and day out, shedding a tear each hour, each day.

> *I was composed at your funeral. I did not share a tear. The worst—watching you go—was over. I find you now invisibly present. You influence my thoughts and my days. I still love you.*

Don't attempt to control or reshape your emotions out of fear that you might hurt other survivors, lose control, be misunderstood or seen by others as vulnerable.

—**Stephen Jamison, Ph.D.** in *Final Acts of Love*

Saying Goodbye

Many folks can stay emotionally involved and present with the dying person while also grieving in anticipation of death.

> I know that hoping for your recovery was foolish. I did not at first believe you were dying. I tried to help you get better, wanting to wish away the inevitable—your death. When you took my hand and said, "I want to go," I knew I would have to face the truth—a future without you. I had to start planning to be without you. But I never will say, "Goodbye."

We said goodbye. But to anybody who ever knew him, he is still alive.

—John Gunther in *Death Be Not Proud*

Life Review

The dying may enjoy looking through photographs of their lives. Sharing memories with people that mean the most to you helps everyone find closure. Joining a loved one in a life review facilitates anticipatory grieving.

> *The nurse told me you talked a lot about the kids and might enjoy seeing our family albums. Looking at the photos, we cried together. Tears of joyful remembrance. Tears of bittersweet sorrow. I'm glad you got to see the photographs one last time.*

Both you as a family member and your dying loved one will mourn in anticipation of death.

—Therese A. Rando, Ph.D. in
How to Go on Living When Someone You Love Dies

Breaking The News

Sometimes it is the person who is dying who breaks the news to family. The dying speak up so the separation can begin. Sometimes the dying wait to cross over until they can arrange for others to care for the loved ones left behind.

> *When you said, "Goodbye," I said, "No." I could not let go of you. You said I'd be all right. You had asked friends and family to help me. You spent your energy helping me cope with losing you.*

To me, it is extraordinary how few people recognize the bereavement that the dying face.

—**Patricia Weenolsen, Ph.D.** in *The Art of Dying*

Care And Support

Families often start to shift relationships and duties when one member is dying. Children often assume a vigilant watch and care for the parent left behind.

> *I see how you arranged for the children to take over the household chores you had always performed. You never stopped thinking of my welfare.*

No matter how convinced you might be that no one can understand or help, it is so imperative that you have support.

—John W. James and Frank Cherry in
The Grief Recovery Handbook

Awkward Planning

When someone we love is dying, we feel awkward planning for the future. We worry that others will judge us as callous when we go on with our own life.

> People said I was heartless when I planned for a future without you. I knew I was doing the things you wanted me to do to keep our family unit together.

The practical aspect of grief is that life must go on, and we must have the courage to redefine our place in the shifting landscape of existence.

—Deanna Edwards in
Grieving: The Pain and the Promise

The Dying Grieve, Too

Dying persons also grieve. They have lost the futures they planned. Family and friends mourn not only the loss of the person, but also the loss of shared hopes and dreams.

> *You left my world when we had plans for us. I turn a corner, and seeing your favorite travel books, you enter my mind. The trips we hoped to take together are not forgotten.*

There will be times when you turn a corner and suddenly you are confronted by a reminder of your deceased loved one.

—Helen Fitzgerald in *The Mourning Handbook*

Toasting With The Family

Living with a dying person feels like riding a roller coaster that you cannot get off. You must hang on until it is over. Only then can you stop to rest, relax and remember.

> *At your funeral, all the remaining aunts, uncles and cousins got together. Everyone told stories about you. There were many toasts to you. We celebrated your life.*

Happiness is the capacity to open the heart and eyes and spirit and be where we are and find happiness in the midst of it. Even in the place of difficulty, there is a kind of happiness that comes if we've been compassionate, that can help us through it.

—Jack Kornfield in *1325 Buddhist Ways to be Happy*

Chapter Five
Remembrance and Contemplation of the Missing Piece

Remembering

In the rising of the sun
And in its going down,
We remember them.

In the blowing of the wind
And in the chill of winter,
We remember them.

In the opening of buds
And in the warmth of summer,
We remember them.

In the rustling of the leaves
And the beauty of the autumn,
We remember them.

In the beginning of the year
And when it ends,
We remember them.

259

When we are lost,
And sick at heart,
We remember them.

So long as we live they, too, shall live.
They are a part of us now,
As we remember them.

Adapted from *The Yiskor*

Sometimes it just takes hearing a story to begin to believe in a new form of consciousness between spirits, alive and dead. St. John Chrysostom prompts us to adopt such thinking when he says, "They whom we love and lose are no longer where they were before. They are now wherever we are."

Stories abound that help us understand contemplation. An ancient tale tells us of the monk who went to the mountain for 40 days and 40 nights. When he descended, the villagers asked him, "What did you learn in all this time away from civilization?" The monk answered, "I ate when I was hungry and slept when I was tired."

The crowd was not satisfied and said, "But, Master, we all eat when we are hungry and we all sleep when we are tired. How was your experience different from our everyday life?"

The monk answered, "People eat more than they need to satisfy their many tastes. People have trouble sleeping because their minds are full of ceaseless thoughts."

The monk took the path of contemplation to better understand himself. Similarly, we all need to carve out a spiritual existence to balance the wear and tear our busy society takes on our bodies. We, like the monk, need to get away from the world to think about what is basic and important in life. We need to take time to think and reflect. We need to carve out time to understand ourselves. Life is meant to be a journey we travel in order to know ourselves and our relationship to all things.

We all need to look at who we really are in this world. Are we at the place we wish to be? The wise know not to judge themselves by how they look. Looks are fleeting. Are we doing what we think is important? Whose company do we choose to keep? What relationships are important to us? We cannot learn using society's mirrors, for they portray a temporal self, not a spiritual one. We must separate ourselves from the world and contemplate using our own mirror to reveal the spiritual being that is truly us.

Death sometimes is the only thing that stops our frenetic day-to-day pace. Death makes us stand still and contemplate the reason for our being and our circumstances in life. Death shakes our world upside down as it snatches a loved one away.

Impermanence is the message death brings. Every day the sun rises and sets over a world whose players are different from the day before. The earth and its inhabitants change from the time the moon waxes to when it wanes. Caterpillars morph into butterflies. Seasons come and go. Birds migrate. Tides flow in and out, ever altering the shoreline and its oceanic inhabitants.

The temporary sanctuary our bodies provide becomes nothing more than fluids and dust. We ask, "Have we been in the center or on the periphery of other people's lives? Did we star in our own story?" We ask, "Will anyone remember us?"

We are remembered by how we actually lived, not by how we say we have conducted our lives. Once death meets us, we no longer can bluff, cajole, charm or bully people into believing we are someone we are not. We cannot hide behind our many educational degrees or business success. We are unmasked.

Our lives are cobbled together much like pieces of a jigsaw puzzle. One section represents our childhood, another our home, another our work experiences. One piece depicts our mother. Another our father. Siblings, relatives and friends—each becomes a piece of our puzzle.

There is a picture on every jigsaw puzzle. It takes time and effort to put the pieces together to create the full image. Likewise, our lives evolve, and our relationships and experiences are the pieces that make us who we are.

When a loved one dies, we lose a piece of our life's puzzle. We still can see a whole picture of the puzzle and imagine the missing piece. We see what we remember.

Some people think that when people leave our every-day lives, they are no longer with us. But we carry these people with us. Just as taking "no action" is essentially taking an action, "non-being" is still being. When people are no longer with us physically, they continue to influence us.

When someone dies, I often cut out a puzzle shape and send it with my sympathy card. The design I make on the surface can be simple or intricate. The color can be bold or pastel. The piece can be cut and curved in such a way that you could tell it would touch more than one piece if placed in the puzzle. My accompanying note says, "This puzzle piece represents your lost loved one. Even though this person is no longer on earth, you know him by his/her absence. Let this puzzle piece be a sign that you carry him/her wherever you go. When you touch the piece, when you look at its shape, its color and its texture, you will be reminded of how this person is captured in your heart, mind and life, even today, though gone from this life. Carry this puzzle piece in your pocket to remind yourself that your loved one continues to fill a space in your life, now and forever. Let your remembrances of your lost loved one beautify your life."

Just when you are convinced that nothing is permanent, you find yourself daydreaming about a long-lost loved one. You thought you had grieved enough to erase your memory. But always you can see in your mind the missing puzzle piece. As we contemplate our precious few years, we can bring into our minds the missing puzzle pieces of our lives.

You may ask just what goes on in the mind of someone who contemplates, like the monk in our story, someone who lets go of everyday life. Is the mind quiet? Is the mind full of random thoughts?

Here are a few steps that may help you reach a contemplative state. Let thoughts pass in and out of your mind. Be present to yourself and the energy around you. Let spirits in. Talk to them. Find some soothing background sounds:

- music
- drumming
- singing birds
- harp

The capacity for remembrance comes from the ability to just let go and "be." The way to complete our grieving is to contemplate the spirit of the loved one lost. The more we can remember and celebrate the spirit of the person, the more we understand that the spirit form is real and eternal. Our loved one cannot be lost to death.

The ultimate aim of remembrance is to bridge a union with our loved one. Remembering relieves us of guilt by acknowledging the external connection that binds us one to another. Remembering strengthens us because we truly realize that it matters not if one's spirit is seen or unseen. The connection remains. Spiritual ties are not broken by death.

We can move ourselves into a remembrance state of consciousness and experience the mystery and wonder of the spiritual realm. We need not stop forever in an acceptance stage whose time has already passed. Relationships are indelible experiences. Be still and you will experience things invisible.

Only *you* will know if you have reached your destination of better knowing yourself and the relationships you can have with people near and dear to you, both deceased and alive.

Contemplation

Contemplative prayer is intended interaction with the world outside our form of being on earth. In contemplation, we detach from images of the world around us. We let go of our ego and all its accompanying day-to-day worries. We just stop thinking of life on earth. In doing so, we open ourselves to the radiant presence of the universe. We open our hearts to fully receive. When we let go, we allow that which is unconscious to us in our daily life come to the forefront of our minds. This is contemplative prayer.

> *I try to get away from this busy world around me. I sit in silence. I hear my breathing. I listen for a long time as I breathe in and out. In paying attention to my breathing, I find I am transported from this world to a place where I can just be and rest. Here I know nothing, think nothing. I just am. I let myself be. When I emerge to re-enter the stream of consciousness, I wonder if where you are now is similar to where I have just been. A quiet place. A place of peace. A place to rest.*

If your mind is empty, it is always ready for anything; it is open to everything. For if we listen with a silent mind, as free as possible from the clamor of preconceived ideas, a possibility will be created for the truth of the teachings to pierce us, and for the meaning of life and death to become increasingly and startling clear.

—Suzuki Roshi in Sogyal Rinpoche's
The Tibetan Book of Living and Dying

Times Of Reflection

Each of us needs to experience our contemplative dimension. At regular times and places, we must put aside our roles in this fast-paced world and create a sacred space in which to think and just "be." When we daily engage our spiritual self, we can have the strength to build lives of charity, integrity and peace.

> *Since you died, I have been alone with my thoughts a lot. This has not been a sad predicament. Instead, during these times of reflection I have renewed my faith in what I believe, what I am willing to stand up for, and what my life is all about. I am determined to give love to those you loved. I am at peace knowing I can do this as you would have wanted.*

We must learn to balance the material wonders of technology with the spiritual demands of our human nature.

—John Naisbitt in *Megatrends*

Silent Meditation

Meditation does not always come easy. Yet one cannot overestimate the power gained by removing oneself from the trivialities of the day. We are all in a hurry to get somewhere else. Be where you are. To give oneself the gift of a space and time to think is necessary if we are to make sense of our existence.

> *Throughout the day, I find my thoughts of you are silenced by trivialities. Cell phone songs grab air space. Work, shopping and planning take up time. I know that life is really all about what happens inside of me. Yet, I, too, as others, fight to keep up with the fast-paced drummer. Now and again, I must sit aside your graveside and talk. I must silence outside life to connect with what is inside me.*

Silence recalls the spirit. It allows for a period when the pandemonium in our lives can be collected, bracketed, put aside. "Spirituality" means living in the spirit and refers to the quality of spiritual presence we can receive into our lives.

—edited by Richard Bell and Barbara L. Battin in *Seeds of the Spirit: Wisdom of the Twentieth Century*

Understanding

It is easy to look at others and say their lives are sad because they are lazy or have not made good decisions in life. How quickly we can judge. How much harder it is for us to be silent and not offer an opinion about the goodness or badness of a situation. Until man meets the road of his own sorrow, he can only glimpse another man's troubled plight. Understanding grows out of experiencing the depths of our own blues. How many roads must we travel down to make us understand that each of us experiences personal sorrows? We tend to be myopic about tragedy, only ruminating about our own. With grace, we can be open and loving to others as they pass through their tough times.

> *I stand here alone. I have walked many roads. The roads have had their twists and turns. Along the way, I was led to you. You became a big part of my life. There are many roads in life a man can walk down. But no better a teacher of love than the journey I had with you.*

People get into situations they never wanted to get into. And it's hard getting out. That's all that is human—the need to lean on something while we stumble through life.

—**Belva Plain** in *Evergreen*

Destiny

Follow the stars wherever they take you. As children, we are told by our parents that the whole world lies out there awaiting us. Our destiny depends on how we see the world and the choices we make. A wise man once said that he who wants to live in peace must, at times, keep his opinion to himself and not judge all he sees.

> *I look at the stars and wonder. I cannot judge the choices you made. I cannot speak for you. I can only talk of what I know. I know your life and mine intersected. The life you now lead is hidden from me by a veil. Someday I will join you and learn the rest of your story.*

To attain true knowledge and wisdom, we must remain open and empty, allowing ideas from others to rush in.

—**Al Huang and Jerry Lynch in**
Mentoring the Tao of Giving and Receiving Wisdom

The Significance Of Our Being

If we had only one life to live, what would its purpose be? Should we strive to create a work of significance? Or should we concentrate on just being and appreciating life? Each person contributes in some way to life. One person's life ripples through the days and nights of others' lives. As we go on, we constantly choose the life we want to live.

> *I think of you and wonder if I was a bit actor in your life or, if in the scheme of things, I was a main character. You brought a lot into my life. I am hoping I brought as much to yours. I am tied to you.*

I have always felt that the action most worth watching is not at the center of things but where the edges meet.

—Anne Fadiman in
The Spirit Catches You and You Fall Down

Chance

All that we have is life. We are all willing to give parts of our lives to others. We have only this one chance to give of ourselves.

> *Chance took you away. But I refuse to live the rest of my life without you. That part of me that also is part of you lives on. I think about "we." We will always exist somewhere beyond this time and space.*

You may give them your love but not your thoughts, for they have their own thoughts. You may house their bodies but not their souls, for their souls dwell in the house of tomorrow, which you cannot visit, not even in your dreams.

—Khalil Gibran

Our Moments

We all become busy. Sometimes so busy we do not stop to think about what life is all about. We get swept away into worldly pursuits of happiness. Our own "to do" list seems most important. And then death interrupts our life to ask, "What are you doing with each precious day?" Suddenly we slow down.

> *I think of all the things we planned. I wonder if I spent all the time I could together with you. Although you are not here in a physical sense, you are influencing how I think and act at this very moment.*

Why has the pleasure of slowness disappeared?

—**Milan Kundera** in *Slowness*

Seeing Through

Because you cannot see things does not mean they do not exist. Sound, intuition, and memory ... can you see them? The time has passed when science must be able to quantify something for people to believe it is real. So it is with relationships. They exist, even if we cannot see them.

> *I am here. You are wherever. We are together today, tomorrow and forever. That's the way it will always be.*

In Edward White's book, The Unobstructed Universe, he wrote of a theory that those who love and pass on are still in the same place that we occupy "just live at a different frequency." He used a fan to illustrate. When an electric fan is stationary, we cannot see through the blades, but if we plug it in and step it up to a high frequency, we can see through the fan.

—Norman Vincent Peale in William Elliott's
Tying Rocks to Clouds: Meeting with Wise and Spiritual People

The Light Of Memories

The memories we make last a lifetime and beyond. Good memories can be sewn into the pockets of our lives and taken out whenever we want to smile.

> *I hold you close in my memories. Good memories console me.*

Feeling light within, I walk.

—**Navajo Night Chant**

274

Wondering Why

The saying, "only the good die young," is meant to capture the belief that people live their time on earth until they understand what they were put on earth to attain. At this point, the person transitions to a higher level of being.

I wonder aloud to myself, "Why is this so? Was this the time you were meant to die? What am I here to learn?" Your death has taught me to think beyond everyday life to the purpose of my being. I am uncertain, searching each day to make meaning out of your life and mine.

We hope that we can grasp by the end of our earthly lives the meaning for our being here.

—Words carved on a totem pole, Vancouver, Canada

Part Of A Bigger Picture

Your true self is composed of who you think you are, who you want others to think you are, and who you really are. Death of a loved one can cause a person to examine their true self. This exploration often enables people to see the awesome, bigger picture of life. This knowledge is humbling.

> *I never understood before your death the awesome transition that occurs when we die. Your death has made me a humbler person. God has a plan.*

Know that grief will change you regardless of whether you want to or not. You can't prevent change. It is part of surviving loss.

—**Stephen Jamison in** *Final Acts of Love*

Precious Time

We are led to believe in this over-commercialized world that the people with many things are better off than the people with few things. Things—all the stuff we have—consume our time. If we have it, we need to care for it. Give the device new batteries. Buy more chemicals for the spa or pool. Dry-clean the fancy clothes. Things get in the way of us spending time on what really matters—our relationships with family and friends and God.

> *When I look back, I wonder if I gave you enough of my time. Many things got in the way of my spending all the time I could with you. I want you to know that now I wish I had put more things aside to be with you.*

Please forgive me.
I forgive you.
Thank you.
I love you.

—**Ira Byock** in *The Four Things That Matter Most*

Our Own Journey

Life's journey lasts forever. We each walk down our own path. The struggles and pain we experience shape who we become. By listening to the voices within us and being honest with ourselves, we identify what we truly feel. We come to know who we are. In stillness, we understand our true being, which will go on forevermore.

> *In quiet times, I dialogue with you. I imagine I am sending and you are receiving my words. I am, like you, a spirit who is trying to make sense of all that has happened. For a time I will inhabit this body. I have faith that later there will be no divide between your spirit and mine.*

It is not an easy journey, but what a worthwhile journey it is. Because the further we proceed in diminishing our narcissism, our self-centeredness and sense of self-importance, the more we discover ourselves becoming not only less fearful of death, but also less fearful of life.

—**M. Scott Peck** in
Further Along the Road Less Traveled

Sharing Ourselves

Sometimes when a loved one dies, we wish we had taken more time to share who we really are with the person. Many times, we let others think what they will about us. Then, when someone important to us dies, we often regret not having shared more of our true self.

> *Who knows me well? Only me. Even you, someone I held close, only knew the person I was before. Your death has reshaped me into the person I am today. I will meet up with you again, and then I will open up more of myself to you.*

I am seeking perhaps what Socrates asked for in the prayer from Phaedrus when he said, "May the outward and inward man be one."

—**Anne Morrow Lindbergh in** *Gift From The Sea*

Forgiveness

Life gives us no choice but to go on. We cannot live in the past. Forward is the only direction available to us. We take our past life along with us because we are changed by what we experienced.

> *Your death has made me face my own weaknesses and forgive myself for not always being strong. I try to stop the tears before they start. This is difficult because I miss you. I want you to know your death has made me more aware of the feelings of others. Now I am more understanding than I was before of the weaknesses of others.*

Forgiveness is the overcoming of negative affect and judgment toward the offender, not by denying ourselves the right to such affect and judgment, but by endeavoring to view the offender with compassion, benevolence, and love while recognizing that he or she has abandoned their right to them.

—Robert D. Enright, Elizabeth A. Gassin and Ching-RuWu in *Forgiveness: A Developmental View*

Years Of Fading Sunset

Death stretches us to our limit. Death changes our lives forever. Death calls us to look beyond ourselves and to reach toward another level of existence.

> *I used to be caught up in all the burdens of life, giving more time to taking care of my possessions than to taking care of my soul. But your death has made me realize that I should spend less time collecting treasures on earth and more time cultivating my spirit—the everlasting part of me.*

Oh, Great Spirit, whose voice I hear in the winds,
And whose breath gives life to all the world—
Hear me.

I come before you, one of your many children.
I am small and weak.
I need your strength and wisdom.

Let me walk in beauty, and make my eyes ever behold
The red and purple sunset.
Make my hands respect the things you have made,
My ears sharp to hear your voice.
Make me wise so that I may know the things
You have taught my people,
The lesson you have hidden in every leaf and rock.

I seek strength
Not to be superior to my brother,
But to be able to master myself.

Make me ever ready to come to you
With clean hands and straight eyes,
So when life fades as a fading sunset,
My spirit may come to you without shame.

—Chief Yellow Lark, Lakota Sioux

Peacefulness Counts

What we become as we walk through all the days of our lives is what counts. There are no points given in the end for the education we have been privileged to receive, the money we counted as ours, the possessions we owned, or the status that was connected to our jobs. What we become, irrespective of these fortunes, is the measure of our soul.

> *You knew so much about the real issues of life ... love, honesty, caring and giving. I wonder, when my day comes, if I will be happy with the person I have become. Or will I be ashamed? Your death makes me think about these things.*

The secret of bringing peace on earth is to remember that whatever peace you bring must begin on that little piece of earth where you live.

—J. Donald Walters in
Secrets of Bringing Peace on Earth

Walking Through Life's Joys and Woes

Life contains a good measure of suffering. We can wade through the suffering, taking with us the lessons it teaches. Or we can be corroded by the misery and become one of the living dead, who each day bemoans its fate, becoming less, not more.

> *I know I am not the only one to lose someone so dear. Indeed, I recognize this as the human condition. I want you to know, however, that whatever happens in my life, part of the reason I go forward is that I feel you would want me to do so.*

It is right it should be so;
Man was made for Joy and Woe;
And when this we rightly know;
Thro' the World we safely go.
Joy and woe are woven fine,
A Clothing for the soul divine.

—William Blake

Examining Life

Some people never live their lives at all. They just follow the prevailing social patterns. People would do well to learn to be who they really are and sing their own song while they are alive.

> *Your death has made me examine my life. I look inside. There is too much to think about and too much to ignore. I am afraid that what I have found inside is less than I want to be. Blinded by pride, passion, envy, laziness, anger and greed, I have not become who I thought I could be. I heard it's never too late to begin again. Please guide me to be more than I am now.*

You had to decide: Am I going to change the world, or am I going to change me? Or maybe change the world a little bit, just by changing me?

—Sarah Louise Delany and Annie Elizabeth Delany in *Having Our Say*

Ownership

We are all renters. Some believe they own parcels and beachfront, townhouses, and mansions. But we are all just passing through. Impermanence is a reality of the human condition. Our years on this earth are a precious few, not to be wasted.

> *I planned on you being here longer. The timing of your death stunned me. I would give anything I own to be with you again. I am thinking about life differently since you died. I wonder if I am living out my time on earth as well as I can. I do good things for people to honor you. Honoring you has become a way of being for me.*

People do not own.

— Judith Simmer-Brown in
Buddhists Reflect on the Rule of Benedict

Believing In Prayer

The essence of prayer is just being. Prayer is not mystical. The specific words we use are less important than the readiness of our heart to listen. Words do not connect us. Being open and aware connects us to the Almighty One. Even if we say nothing and sit in silence, resting, away from the world in our interior self and detached from thoughts of day-to-day activities, we experience a connection with a Great Spirit. When we allow ourselves to say, "Come, I am ready to connect with you," prayer will naturally happen.

> *I sit in silence and allow the spiritual realm in. I find it hard to express in words this state I am in. I'm not reaching out with words of prayer and salutations. But I am open to you reaching me. I know this is where I belong.*

Prayer is not asking. It is a longing of the soul.

—Gandhi

Opening Oneself To Receiving

Some people describe prayer as a tranquil presence. The person praying has no agenda other than to be open and receiving. Prayer allows God and the spiritual world in.

> *Your death has taught me about life. Where before I was in denial of what there could be beyond this life, I am now a believer.*

Death is not the extinguishing of the light, but merely the turning down of the lamp now that the dawn has come.

—Rabindranath Tagore, Bengali Poet

Simple Prayer

Prayer is not a way to cajole God into making things happen for us. Life will happen the way it is meant to. Prayer brings peace when it allows those who pray to acknowledge, "Thy will—not my will—be done."

> *I often pray. I pray because I think only God can really understand the deep gash your death has made in my heart. I go to a quiet spot and just rest in God.*

Perfect prayer is not to know that you are praying.

—Thomas Keating in *Open Mind, Open Heart*

The State Of Unconditional Love

There is personal freedom in being more accepting of others. No longer must we judge. No longer must we defend. We can just give unconditional love.

> Some days when this world spins too fast, I wonder what it is like to be free like you. Some people may say you left life far too early. But my heart tells me you found a better place. For this I am grateful.

An Old Celtic Prayer

You are the pure love of the clouds.
You are the pure love of the skies.
You are the pure love of the stars.
You are the pure love of the moon.
You are the pure love of the sun.
You are the pure love of the heavens.
You are the pure love of each living creature.
You are the pure love of the Creator of all life.

—Thomas Cowan in
Shamanism: A Spiritual Practice for Daily Life

My Own Offenses

Deaths through accidents that are not preventable are easier to understand than deaths due to risky behavior.

> *You chose to live your life in a way that did not always make sense to me. I think differently from you. I understand everyone has a right to choose their own way. I wonder what you would be thinking about me if I had been the one who died.*

That I feed the hungry, forgive an insult, and love my enemy—these are great virtues. But what if I should discover that the poorest of beggars and the most impudent of offenders are all within me, and that I stand in need of alms of my own kindness; that I myself am the enemy who must be loved—what then?

—Carl Jung

Knowing

The world is a crazy place and we know it. Atrocities have undoubtedly occurred throughout the ages. But before, they were oceans and continents away. With instant media coverage, we can no longer deny what is happening. Now we know. There is no way of not knowing.

> *Now I know what I was too blind to see before. Life is a short, mysterious time. If we are fortunate, we learn how to truly love one another and accept love ourselves. Now I know what I did not know when you were alive. Life is to be embraced. We need to work on making good situations out of bad ones. Once we understand unconditional love, we cannot sit on our hands, but must become activists for a better world. Now I know.*

A basic need of modern man is liberation from his inordinate self-awareness, his obsession with self-affirmation so that he may enjoy the freedom from concern that goes with being simply what he is and accepting things as they are in order to work with them as he can.

—Thomas Merton

The Book Of Our Life

The voice of God often comes to us through tragedies. It is easy to worship God in happy times. It is harder to hear God when we are sad.

> *Before you died, I went to church to worship. The words flowed. I was so good at reciting prayers. Now I may have fewer words to say to God, but I say my own words. I seek a personal relationship with the grace of God to guide me through this rough time.*

Life is God's novel.
Let God write it.

—**Isaac Bashevis Singer**

Reality Check

Are we placed here by chance? Is birth preordained to pass on wisdom, riches or power? Are we just puppets God moves about for entertainment? Are we here to listen and see what each day brings?

> *I thought that if I planned my life well, it would just unfold accordingly. Your death tells me that I was a fool to think I could even see, much less plan, my future. Now I am ready to listen. Now I am ready to believe this world is one part of eternity. My heart tells me you are waiting for me in another part of eternity.*

Keep the reality of death before your eyes—have a care about how you act every hour of your life.

—**Rule of Benedict**

Truths

We remember the heroes of yesterday. We celebrate their lives. Though long dead, each reaches us and touches our lives.

I am thankful for your existence.
Your life taught me a lot.

The dead carry with them to the grave in their clutched hands only that which they have given away.

—DeWitt Wallace

Our Very Best Efforts

It has been said the only worthwhile accomplishments are not those for which we receive the praise of others but the lessons we teach ourselves.

> *I ask myself what my life means. I look at your life for insight. I hope I can learn to be valued by others as you were.*

Many of us live one-eyed lives. We rely largely on the eye of the mind to form our image of reality. But today more and more of us are opening the other eye, the eye of the heart, looking for realities to which the mind's eye is blind. Either eye alone is not enough. We need "wholesight," a vision of the world in which our mind and heart unite "as my two eyes make one in sight." Our seeing shapes our being. Only as we see whole can we and our world be one.

—**Parker Palmer** in *To Know As We Are Known: Education as a Spiritual Journey*

Passing On History

Long ago, wisdom was transferred person-to-person. Families passed on their history and values through storytelling.

> *There are so many things I had yet to tell you. I ask myself if I was clear enough when I tried to explain how I felt, what you meant to me and my hopes for you. Did I take enough time to talk face-to-face with you, or did I let the busyness of the days come between my telling you the stories you needed to know to understand our life together?*

The tragedy of modern man is not that he knows less and less about the meaning of his own life, but that it bothers him less and less.

—**Vaclav Havel in** *Letters to Olga*

Learning As You Go

Families can pass down hurtful ways of treating each other from one generation to the next.

> *I will try to learn from whatever imperfections there were in our relationship. I will treat better those you and I love. I will let this be your legacy.*

People want to make a commitment to a purpose—a goal—a vision that is bigger than themselves.

—**John Naisbitt in *Re-inventing the Corporation***

The Wisdom Of Being

The permanence of impermanence is not an easy concept for people to understand. Society tells us to run at breakneck speed to gain all the material wealth we can, only to have it stripped from us at death.

> *My striving for fame and fortune ended with your death. Instead, now I seek more to understand and to love well. I've gained wisdom. I've gained some hope. I am now more loosely tethered to the earth and more connected through you to the world beyond.*

No race can prosper until it learns that there is as much dignity in tilling a field as in writing a poem.

—Booker T. Washington

Be Open, Think Beyond

In order to understand life beyond, we must follow our intuition. Only if we allow ourselves to be open and think beyond this time and place can we truly know the expanse of time called life.

> *I try each day to become a better person. Your death has revealed to me some intentions of life: to learn, to love, to be just, and to just be.*

He (Buddha) saw the human life form as the evolutionary gateway through which the egocentric individual self-preoccupied life process can enter the realm of selfless energetic love and compassion, artfully surrounding all interconnecting beings in an endlessly benevolent web of beauty and opportunity.

—**Robert Thurman**

Tuned In

Many of the annoyances of this life fade when a person understands that life is preparation for a spiritual existence.

> *I have no energy to get angry in a traffic jam.*
> *Queuing up in a long line no longer makes me mad.*
> *Instead, I take this time to daydream. No amount of*
> *pressure from the outside will take away my*
> *intention to be a beneficent presence on this earth.*

Attentiveness is not tenseness or strained effort
but presence and relaxation, quietness and
receptivity, presence with love. Attentiveness
can be learned. We can become sensitized to
attentiveness.

—**A Carthusian Monk**

Moving Forward

A saying goes, "One sickness, long life. No sickness, short life." This means if people understand what is wrong with them and compensate for their weaknesses, they will live longer than people who consider themselves without flaw and neglect their health.

> *I think understanding is the key to dealing with loss. I understand that I am forever changed. I realize I must accept what has happened and go on. I try to hold good thoughts despite the tragedy of your death. I am not always successful. I move forward to honor you.*

Life is slowly falling forward.

—P. Inman

Just Beyond

We must be willing to pull aside the curtain between life and death in order to embrace what is ours on the other side.

> *There are days when I feel people in this world are in spiritual bankruptcy. They are unable to understand more than the world in which they live. They do not look beyond what they do each day. I cannot give them a glimpse into the place you and I share. They must find it with their own hearts in their own time.*

Since the beginning of history, people have sensed the presence of some spiritual force, the continued existence of which lies at the core of things.

—Daisaku Ikeda in *Unlocking the Mysteries of Birth and Death ... and Everything in Between*

Seeing Who We Want to Be

Some days it is like my brakes are on. I don't go forward. I can't. I take more from people than I give. At the end of the day, I wish I had taken the opportunity to give more. We look back over the lives of people we have known and loved and we ask ourselves, "How small is my contribution in comparison to theirs?" Lives that communicated love. Lives that contributed music. Lives that painted the world a wonderful place to enjoy. How often, in retrospect, are we humbled by the solitary life of one human being?

Your death has taught me I have no time to waste. I want to do things that matter.

The real discovery is not seeking new lands, but in seeing with new eyes.

—**Marcel Proust**

Possessions Don't Define Us

Each of us hides behind fancy clothes, cars and houses while, at the same time, hoping that someday someone will love us for who we truly are.

I know now this life's possessions are imagined. We are all renters and borrowers. Things bought and sold for cash don't last. Nothing but the spirit remains in the end. How gladdened I am that I spent time here with you, and will again recognize and greet you one day.

Imagine no possessions.

—John Lennon

Am I The Person I Want to Be?

"To be nobody-but-yourself in a world which is doing its best, night and day, to make you like everybody else—means to fight the hardest battle any human being can fight; and never stop fighting."

—e.e. cummings

> *Then I did not understand what I do now. You wanted always to be yourself. Your death makes me ask who I am. Am I the person I really want to be?*

Self-knowledge is for the purpose of contributing.

—Alene Moris

Goodness

When we find fault with others, sometimes it is our perception that is the problem.

> *Since your death, I am less quick to criticize others. Situations seem less black and white. I can now understand there is more than one right point of view. You have led me away from sleepwalking through life to the realization that how I look at things is my choice.*

People's goodness or badness is a reflection of the circumstances in which they find themselves.

—**Eldridge Cleaver**

Acceptance Of The Future

People who grieve face not only the loss of a loved one, but also carry with them the burden that a glimpse at mortality brings.

> *Your death has become a sacred wound that has taught me people cannot foresee when they may become vulnerable. I now surrender myself to God's plan and whatever the future holds for me.*

Prayer does not change God, but changes him who prays.

—Søren Kierkegaard

Being Each Others' Angels

Kindness is a stretching of ourselves for others. Kindness goes beyond what is convenient and socially prescribed. In kindness, we move beyond what we must do for others to what we can and will do for those in need. Sometimes it takes being wounded ourselves to understand where our kindness can make a difference in someone's life. It matters how we treat each other.

> *Before your death, I hadn't a clue as to all the hurt people experience in life. Now it's plain to me that we all get hurt, most often through no fault of our own. I realize now that I can be kind to people who are suffering.*

I believe in bands of angels, bands of secular angels.

—**Jean Houston in William Elliott's** *Tying Rocks to Clouds: Meetings and Conversations with Wise and Spiritual People*

Seeking Quietness

For a person to think with their heart, silence is needed.

> *I spend time with my own thoughts of you. If I were to tell other living souls how I talk to you, they would say my words are useless chatter. But for me, thinking with my heart is a way to connect with you.*

If I do not seek quietness around me, I cannot hear the words that my heart whispers. And if I do not seek silences within, I will never know the power of my words as instruments of creation.

—G. Lynn Nelson in *Writing and Being: Taking Back Our Lives through the Power of Language*

Shaping Our Destiny

All men have a destiny carried out through extraordinary circumstances, quite often beyond our control or wisdom. How we respond to this destiny says a lot about who we are.

> *Seeing how your life unfolded, I wonder what my destiny will be. I see now how little control we have over the events we plan for ourselves.*

You are a finely tuned instrument; you know when the call is for you, and when it is not. Then the tasks, the persons, the relationships feel given, and ourselves simply the recipients of the life and energy that is dispensing itself through us.

—Elaine M. Prevallet in *Reflections on Simplicity*

Digging Deep

The work of the heart is to learn about who we are deep inside no matter what the outside circumstances may be.

> *Your death has taught me to look deeply inside myself. I should improve who I am on the inside, for that is what I will carry forward, like you, into the next life.*

But if you want to identify me, ask me not where I live, or what I like to eat, or how I comb my hair, but ask me what I am living for, in detail, and ask me what I think is keeping me from living fully for the thing I want to live for.

—Thomas Merton in Jim Forest's
Living With Wisdom: A Life of Thomas Merton

What Has Meaning For Me?

Life can be described as a journey we travel to get to know who we are. Our friends, families and acquaintances are our teachers. Our experiences are our maps.

I have learned that each decision I make is personal.
I can participate in life as much as I choose.
Embedded in this freedom is the understanding that
I may cast aside the ways of this world as I try to
become the person I want to be. I want to be
someone who would make you proud.

To do good things in the world, first you must know who you are and what gives meaning in your life.

—Paula Brownlee

Living My Religion

You have to stop living up to others' expectations and follow your heart. Cultivate yourself. Synchronize your actions with your intentions. Become the person you always intended to be.

I am happy today because I believe in a world to come. I believe in an afterlife wherein all differences are left at the door and people commune in peace and harmony. To this end, I am trying to live a principled life, to be who I am and who I will be forever.

Worship and living are not two separate realms. Unless living is a form of worship, our worship has no life.

—Abraham Heschel

Inside Each Of Us

Only by partaking in life and interacting with others can people truly understand themselves. We are formed through our interactions with others. Each of us has inside, invisible to the eye, our *true* self.

> *I have wondered of late what I would be like if you had not died. I was so self-assured, thinking life was going my way, as well it should. Now I am more humble. I know circumstances are often beyond my control. And this makes me more understanding of others and the many hardships that befall them. My perception of myself and others has changed dramatically. I have become more loving and accepting.*

It is only with the heart that one can see rightly; what is essential is invisible to the eye.

—Antoine de Saint-Exupéry

One Another

People who know God are more accepting of other people despite their faults and failings. The goal of spiritual practice is to become more like God, who loves all people regardless of their station in life. Loving people unconditionally is not an easy task.

> *I am at peace with our relationship. I have learned too late that I could have been a less critical and more kind presence in your life.*

Empathy is the ability to put oneself emotionally in another's situation—that is, to imagine and perhaps actually to experience the pain of another human being.

—**Kenneth Pelletier, M.D.,** in *Sound Mind, Sound Body*

Rekindling Lights

Each and every person is a messenger of God. We need to be attentive to the people and experiences in our lives and to ask, "Why? Why now? What am I to learn?" Not to listen to the messages in our experiences is to not grow into the person we are meant to be.

> *Your death was a message for me to examine my life. I used to think that what I did was more important than who I was. I was busy, too busy. I was wrapped up in the world. Your death halted my fast-paced life in its tracks. Losing you has made me more conscious of my desire to become a better person each day.*

Sometimes our light goes out but it is blown into flame by another human being. Each of us owes deepest thanks to those who have rekindled this light.

—Albert Schweitzer

Two Views

They say the eyes of the old are watching two worlds.

> *I know that I am not promised tomorrow. Death is a certainty for all of us. Yet, I am grateful for each day because I am coming to know more clearly who I am and what I live for.*

My grandmother cradles a vital fire always.
And, sometimes, I am aware that she will die.

—**Kaia Sand** in *Chants of Wonder*

Spanning Life And Death

Instead of getting to know and understand the spirit we are given in our lifetimes, we put off thoughts of who we are as a spirit until death comes near. Many think that the spirit or soul forms in the afterlife.

> *Now that I have experienced the death of someone I love so dearly, I realize that life and death are not worlds apart. In death, we transform totally into the spirit we have been developing.*

What I need to make me happy in this life is not of this world.

—Joan Chittister, OSB

Lessons Of Experience

Experiences with death deepen our understanding of our spirit.

I have changed in my awareness of the phases of life and in awareness of my spiritual side. For the first time in my life, I understand that I am not going to change into a soul. I already am a soul.

We cannot become what we need to be by remaining what we are.

—**Max DePree in David McNally's**
Even Eagles Need a Push

Learning As We Go

Those who grieve seek answers again and again. But there are no answers. People who say they have all the answers are just making them up. The answers to life's questions do not have to be found. But the questions still need to be asked. Sometimes it is in asking and not finding that the much greater scheme of things appears to us. God has the answers. We shall not have all the answers in this life.

> *I feel like some people judge me harshly. Others feel sympathy for my plight of losing you. Believe me when I say that I have tried not to misstep. I am only human. I do not have the answers. I long to not have agonizing questions continually on my mind.*

If we listened to our intellect, we'd never have a love affair. We'd never have a friendship. We'd never go into business, because we'd be cynical. Well, that's nonsense. You've got to jump off cliffs all the time and build your wings on the way down.

—Ray Bradbury

A Greater Understanding

We must be free to transcend what we have been taught in order to grow beyond our beliefs.

> I used to think that people alone were responsible for how their lives turned out. Now that I am open to a spiritual plane and divine intervention, I am more relaxed. I do not feel that all of my life is up to me. I have been brought to this point in life for a reason. I do not need to know the reason. I just need to appreciate that forces other than my conscious will are at work in my world.

Whatever you do anyway, remember that these things are mysteries and that if they were such that we could understand them, they wouldn't be worth understanding. A God you could understand would be less than yourself.

—Flannery O'Connor

Mysteries

"The most beautiful emotion we can experience is the mystical. It is the source of all true art and science. He to whom this emotion is a stranger, who can no longer wonder and stand rapt in awe, is as good as dead."

—Albert Einstein

Since your death, I am more aware of the holy in my ordinary day. Old words of prayers seem new. I see my day as filled with God's presence. Sometimes God speaks to me through people. God is also revealed to me when I see good works being done by one person for another. At these times, I ask God to help me be the person He calls me to be. I am ready.

Caught up as most of us are in the complex ties of daily living, we forget that we are surrounded by the creative power of love. Every once in a while, we need to step aside from the troubles and pleasures of our lives, and take a fresh look, a time to feel and listen to our source.

—Madeleine L'Engle

Learning About Ourselves

We are privileged to be alive and have time to get to know ourselves and the meaning of life.

> *I will be honest and say I do not know everything. But of this I am sure. Grieving cures the soul of many misconceptions about life and brings a person to the realization that God manifests Himself in all of us. We must look and listen for the awesome connections that serendipitously connect us, that we may grow in understanding, peace and thankfulness.*

Man needs reckless courage to descend into the abyss of himself.

—William Butler Yeats

Love Defines You

It is human nature to examine one's life and one's loves.

> *Now I see that life is a lesson of learning to give love and receive love. Someday I will be face-to-face with love. Love lives on forever.*

Love believes in others. Love will bear all things with hope. Love endures forever.

—I Corinthians 13

Honesty

To be completely honest with oneself takes much effort. Honesty calls for respecting and upholding the truth, being straightforward and sincere. When you find yourself in a spot where you can't say something sincere, just be quiet.

> *I learned that I did not have to know a lot about life and death to go through it. I have gained much knowledge of myself. I understand what it means to support others who are grieving. I learned that silence says a lot. I show my love sometimes by just being present.*

To be completely honest with oneself is the very best effort a human being can make.

—Sigmund Freud

What Remains

When we climb a mountain, the view is entirely different from how it was below. We can see farther. Likewise, when we realize death is an aperture to a spiritual future, our view of life on earth becomes limited by comparison.

> *I no longer worry about the security money can buy in this life. I understand I shall pass, at some time, into a spiritual life where I shall know more. My security comes in knowing I have become the spirit I have chosen to be.*

When you were born, you cried
And the whole world rejoiced.
Live such a life that when you die,
The whole world cries and you rejoice.

—Herman Wouk in *Winds of War*

Love In Action

Things are not always as they appear. Take, for example, whiskey. You see it as a liquid in the glass in which it was poured. But not until you fully imbibe do you find the spirit hidden within.

> *As I explore who I am, I wonder if others see me simply as another person just trying to make my way through life as best I can. Or, am I to others as you are to me, a spirit that communes, that strengthens and inspires? I want to be like a fine wine, full-bodied, with spiritual properties to share.*

Perhaps only a smile, a little visit, the fact of building a fire for someone, writing a letter for a blind person, bringing a few coals, finding a pair of shoes, reading for someone, this is only a little bit, yes, a very tiny bit, but it will be our love of God in action.

—**Mother Theresa of Calcutta**

Good Grief

There is no such thing as empty space. If we can go places now that just exist in our mind, what makes us think these spaces cannot be reached after a death? We can advance to the grief stage of remembrance and not stay trapped in acceptance, whose time has already passed.

> *You exist for me in every room of the house. I picture you at the table. I see you on the lawn. I "bump into you" when I fall asleep at night.*

When a loved one dies, grieving never ceases, it becomes a permanent aspect of life. But at the same time, it can be the activation of a conscious soul life.

—**Robert Sardello in** *Love and the Soul*

Gathered In Secret

You never know when memories are made. Only the people who have those memories know.

> *I can tell that people wish I would just let my memories of you fade and go away. They want me to stop talking about you. I know our memories were made to last forever. Remembering comforts me.*

I believe there is a place where our vanished days secretly gather. The name of that place is memory.

—John O'Donohue in
Anam Cara: A Book of Celtic Wisdom

Good Times

Ordinary life is the fabric of which sacred life is made. The sacred and the secular cannot be divided. We achieve the good life when we live our everyday lives extraordinarily well.

> *I look back at the simple times we shared. In them I see clearly, when before I had not, that our times were a blessing for each of us. I am thankful that we could be together. My memories sustain me.*

As I look back on the part of the mystery which is my own life, my own fable, what I am most aware of is that we receive more than we can ever give; we receive it from the past, on which we drain every breath.

—Edwin Muir in *An Autobiography*

Love Resonating

The golden rule: Treat others as we would want to be treated. To give this kind of love requires we forget about ourselves and focus on someone else. How many of us do that well?

> *Love overwhelms me with thoughts of you. I cry because you died. But I have made up my mind. I am trying to stand tall and be strong. I will reach out today to help another person who also grieves for you. Just as I loved you and you loved me, I will try to give the same love in your name.*

Love one another as I have loved you.

—Jesus

Seeing Ourselves In Others

Forgiveness is a theme in all religions. People need to both feel forgiven, and to forgive.

> *There were times when I wish I had been less judgmental. My heart no longer cares who was right. I hope you forgive me.*

The knowledge that our years are limited makes our choices matter.

—**Harold Kushner** in *How Good Do We Have To Be?: A New Understanding of Guilt and Forgiveness*

Aches And Pains

Grief touches the whole body. Every cell feels the loss. Immunity to disease is dampened.

> *My aches and pains have increased fourfold since you died. People said this might happen. My friends are not surprised. But I want to turn this around. I don't want to be sick. I want to live life fully. I shall do something good in your name. I believe that doing so will strengthen me.*

Illness comes from a gradual blocking of body energy.

—Marie Cargill in
Acupuncture: A Visible Medical Alternative

Still Communicating

The communication we have with others in life can be extended after a person dies.

> *My life now has been divided into two parts. The life I had with you before your death and the relationship I have with you now after your death. I choose to carry you with me. I will never leave you in the past.*

Conversations, communications belong to those willing to take moments to sense and to glimpse into a place larger than the world in which we live.

—Huston Smith in *The Illustrated World's Religions*

Within Each Of Us

The prophet Khalil Gibran said, "I know his father; how do you expect me not to know him?"

There are things I would teach you if you were here with me. Your death has been a revelation for me. I have learned who I am. I remember who I had hoped to be. Somewhere in between, I am me. I hope with all my heart I was good enough for you.

I pray thee, O God, that I may be beautiful within.

—Socrates

Never All Alone

People who grieve oftentimes feel as though they're all alone. But this is not so.

> I was wrong to believe others when they said I must realize you are gone and that this grief would pass. I understand that your form has changed. You exist as a spirit. Today I know, though before I did not believe, that I am still in your presence and you are in mine. I comprehend you in all that is enchanting in life.

An English anthropologist was traveling through a distant land interviewing and studying native people. One night, while camped between villages, he heard drumming. He headed toward it. He found a man dancing around a fire. The man chanted and sang, put down the drum and picked up rattles, and continued his ecstatic movements around the fire. After about an hour of continuous dancing, drumming and rattling, the man sat down to eat. The anthropologist said politely, "Sir, I have been admiring your ritual. Why are you here all alone, dancing, drumming, rattling and chanting? You must tell me what it's all about. What does it all mean?" The native regarded him with a puzzled look and asked, "What do you mean, 'all alone?'"

—Thomas Cowan in
Shamanism as a Spiritual Practice for Daily Life

The Real You

The real victories of our lives are not the money and possessions we acquire or the status we attain in society. The only accomplishments that matter are the victories we win over ourselves and the love we have given away. The things we can count, don't count. The things we cannot count, count.

You helped me understand the significance of being honest with myself and making decisions that would not hurt others. Your life keeps on counting on this earth because you blessed me with your wisdom about what is vital to accomplish in life. You advised me that giving unconditional love and accepting love—even if that love is imperfect—are the most important acts we humans can undertake.

When a child loves you for a long time, not just to play with, but really loves you, then you become real.

—**Margery Williams in** *The Velveteen Rabbit*

Sharing My Thoughts

It is hard to remain strong in the midst of painful life experiences. It is difficult to stay in control when confronted with death that tears from us that which has been a major part of us.

> *I alternate between craving good company that consoles me and seeking solitude in order to think. I try to find a balance somewhere between the two extremes. Allowing only select people to know my true thoughts saves me from trite conversations meant to raise my spirits.*

I live in an American desert, without much company, without television, because I am trying to know where on earth I am.

—**Kathleen Norris** in *Dakota: A Spiritual Geography*

Tears

Tears of grief make us stop and reflect. Tears remind us to take time to think, to treasure, and to be present in the moment.

> *I cry seeing an old man struggle across the traffic lanes in time to make the change of the light. I weep when I see a young man and his child buying flowers on Mother's Day. My eyes water when I see someone your age having fun with friends. Tears flow for all sorts of reason: tears of remembering joy that once was, and tears in recognition of shared emotions. Tears are a secret space where I sometimes meet you.*

The more we keep our spontaneity in check when responding, the more extinct it may become.

—**Bruno Bettelheim** in *The Informed Heart*

Less Is More

The old tale of a man and a frog: A man walks by a frog who says, "Please pick me up and kiss me." The man looks away and walks on. The frog hops fast to catch up to the man. The frog yells, "If you kiss me, I will become a beautiful princess for you to have and to hold." The man looks down and picks up the frog. He places the frog in his pocket and walks on. The frog screeches to get the man's attention, "Remember, if you kiss me, I will become a beautiful princess." The man looks into his pocket and says, "Appearances are deceiving. I think a talking frog is more entertaining."

> *Things may not be as they seem. I go through my day and many things in life are sweet. But nothing is quite as wonderful as reflecting on our love.*

Life is really pretty good most of the time, so long as I remember to keep looking at it that way.

—**Ann Patchett** in *Truth & Beauty: A Friendship*

Dead, Not Gone

People matter forever. Their stories need not end at death. Everyone needs to know that they matter to others.

> *You mattered to me. I will carry your story forward.*
> *I must not stop talking about you. I will not let your*
> *story go untold.*

It turns out that human beings reason largely
by means of stories, not by mounds of data.

—**Leah L. Curtin, Editor**
Nursing Management, **Vol. 25 #11**

Only Love

Love is an attitude of the heart.

> *I feel your love and your presence.*
> *I know I will be with you again.*

"The bridge is love," the poet said, "the only
survival, the only meaning."

—**Ellen Gilchrist in** *The Anna Papers*

In My Heart

People who die remain in the hearts and minds of those who live on.

I remain certain of your existence in a world beyond.
I reminisce and then return to the tasks of my life, rejuvenated.

If I leave, it doesn't mean I love you any less.
Keep me in your heart for a while.

—**Warren Zevon in "The Wind"**

Sacred Places

It is important that those who grieve have a ceremonial place where they can unload their heavy hearts and talk to the person who has died. Some people do this at a cemetery. Others make a home altar upon which they place a picture of the deceased along with memorabilia such as letters, readings, and favorite flowers. Mourners may burn incense and candles in honor of their loved one. People who grieve may set out traditional foods and drink to show the lost loved one respect.

> *We have lined up pictures of you on our fireplace mantle. We have placed your favorite plant there also, along with some notes you wrote. It is comforting to have this place for remembering you in our home. This space is a sacred place. You still remain very much with us.*

When I am old and my body has begun to fail me, my memories will be waiting for me.

—**Kent Nerburn** in *Simple Truths*

Connecting Again

Hug meditation consists of taking hold of a person you love, breathing in and out for three full breaths, while being present only to this person. Enjoy your feelings.

Sometimes it is hard for me to connect with other people. It is almost as if I am afraid to again love someone as much as I loved you. I promise to hug someone today. I will be present in the hug.

A happy person is not a person with a certain set of circumstances but rather a person with a certain set of attitudes.

—Hugh Downs in David McNally's
Even Eagles Need a Push

Room For Gladness

One day a traveler asked a monk if he could teach him about truth. The monk said, "Sit here and be quiet and you will learn." The traveler sat and thought all day long. At the end of the day, he came to the monk and said, "I do not think I have learned anything." "Come for tea," said the monk. The monk poured the traveler a cup of tea and, as he did so, continued to pour until the cup overflowed with tea. "Stop," cried the traveler. "Why are you doing this? Look what you have done." The monk said to the traveler, "You are like this cup of tea. You will not learn about truth until you empty out your thoughts and be open to new learning."

> *Your death filled me with grief. I could not think about anything else. I was lost until I realized that I could reframe our relationship in terms of a spiritual one. Now I see every day as time when I can fill myself with good memories of you and me. I just had to make space to remember you with gladness.*

Life itself, when understood and utilized for what it is, is sweet.

—**Benjamin Hoff** in *The Tao of Pooh*

My Choice

Suffering can be a great teacher. Sickness, aging, and death force us to see there is a spirit that transcends this life. This lesson may be the hardest concept we need to grasp during our time on earth.

> *I know I must focus on the future. I have a choice in front of me. I can't look behind all the time. I will live my belief that you are a spirit. I cannot see you, but you are there. My heart and mind feel your presence and carry you with me each day.*

The greatest discovery of my generation is that human beings can alter their lives by altering their attitude of mind.

—**William James**

Making My Life Goals

By understanding life is a transient state of being, we can choose better how we want to spend the days we have. Those who know death cherish each moment.

> I understand nothing stays the same. This has been made more apparent to me by your death. I am running out of time to do the things I want to do with my life. I stand up. I look around. I make my choices. Your death has shown me that sometimes a person needs to change the direction of their life. Now I see myself as someone who is focused on some goals that will complete me. There are only so many days to serve on this earth.

To do things beautifully, to handle ugly problems beautifully, with a deep regard for the sacredness of the human status—that is the Divinity in each of us.

—Pir Vilayat Inayat Khan in *Awakening*

Taking You Along

We each have to learn from our experiences of losing people we love. Otherwise, our difficulties are truly meaningless.

Sometimes I think I am just rolling along, never recovering from your death as people say I should. "When will you get over him?" they ask. "Never," I say. I meet you every day in some way. The memories. The pictures in my mind. You are with me still.

Life can only be understood backwards, but it must be lived forwards.

—**Søren Kierkegaard**

Echoes Of You

Beneath our feet, we can hear the echoes of our minds.

> *We hiked together a lot. Now when I walk, my mind plays over and over again the adventures we shared. It is good to remember those times. Sad, but also good.*

We couldn't be quiet at the table because we had stories to tell. We were planning together. We were in the future together.

—**David J. Chalmers** in *The Conscious Mind: In Search of a Fundamental Theory*

Shine On

Think of yourself as a stone in a polishing tumbler. You get bounced around. You fall. You fly. You tumble. Whether you get crushed or you come out like a polished gem depends a whole lot on who you are inside.

> *When you died, I thought I would never heal. So deep was the emptiness inside me. And then I searched into the depths of myself and found someone who does not give up, who wants to move forward, who enjoys and helps people, and who loves you forever. Without suffering, maybe I would never have learned that I had these qualities. I surprised myself and emerged from grief, a person who again could glow. I gave up my anger. I began to smile at people again. I sang along with others. I joined in reverie. I bet this makes you happy.*

The theme of "broken bones heal the strongest" offers a much-needed antidote to the cultural whine that traumatic or difficult periods of life weaken the body and mind.

—James Fries, M.D., in Kenneth Pelletier's
Sound Mind, Sound Body

Graveside

Many want their remains to be placed in the earth. Families and friends may then gather at the graveside to share words and remember the good times.

> *People ask why I go to your graveside to talk to you. I go because I feel you touch me there. Words cannot express clearly the connection I feel. People need to trust me and understand that I must go.*

She was no longer wrestling with the grief, but could sit down with it as a lasting companion and make it a sharer in her thoughts.

—George Eliot

Restoring Relationships

We all have the need for physical and spiritual nourishment. Food boosts our energy. Sleep rests our minds and bodies. Relationships restore our spirit.

> *I talked with your brother today. He spends more time at the house with me now that you are gone from here. We've become better friends. Our relationship strengthens me.*

The ornament of a house is the friends who frequent it.

—Ralph Waldo Emerson

Memorable Places

Some things are unforgettable.

> *I look at your photograph. Although it does not capture all of you, it reminds me of good times we had together. Some days I just like picking up some pictures of us and remembering. It does me good.*

If you could tell the story of your life by taking someone a half-dozen places, where would you go?

—John Kotre in
White Gloves: How We Create Ourselves in Memory

Choosing

Our eyes behold the dawn. We bow down in honor. Or at least we should. No day should be too busy to honor the mystery of the day, no day too full to walk without heart.

> *I get up. I say to myself, "Another day without you." My body wants to curl back up into bed. And then I realize my duty to meet the day, with all its uncertainties. Each day is a day I will try to fully experience, not just get through. I will smile at the person who is sad. I will have patience with the person whose presence is unpleasant. I will try hard to make this day worth my being here.*

Value your feelings. Let your feelings be a part of the decision-making process.

—**Art Ulene** in *Feeling Fine*

Keeping The Beauty That Is You

Our lives may be broken and saddened by things beyond our control.

> *I am being asked by many to put you behind me.*
> *They say that only then can I get back to life as*
> *normal. But I cannot forget my good times with you.*
> *I shall forevermore connect with you. That is just*
> *the nature of the bond between you and me.*

Nature does not know extinction; all it knows is transformation.

—Wernher Von Braun

Healing Time

You can tell when someone is healing and feeling stronger after experiencing the death of a loved one. The person remembers and talks about their loved one without crying. The person makes new friends. The person has the energy and inclination to give of themselves to others again.

I know I am healing. I can tell stories about you without feeling uncomfortable. My favorite screensaver is a picture with you in it. I have become friends with people with whom I never imagined I would have anything in common. I have the energy to get to know people. I am seeing and acting on opportunities to help others. People tell me I am nice to be around. Thank you for helping me with the strength I need to be all I want to be in this life now.

Sometimes, I have found, one must wait a long time for exactly the right moment.

—**Norman Fischer** in *Benedict's Dharma: Buddhists Reflect on the Rule of Saint Benedict*

Stumbling On Life's Lessons

"Miracles may indicate that our growth as human beings is assisted by a force other than our conscious will."

—St. Augustine

> *Your death has taught me many things. I realize that we each have a choice in how we see the world. I understand that I can love someone who prefers a path different from my own. I need to let others follow their hearts. One day, when I had other plans, you died. After the numbness and the anger wore off, I began to stumble onto lessons. I am healing. I am loving people more. As I move forward, I take you with me.*

Seventy-three percent of Americans surveyed said they believed in miracles.

—A. Greeley in *Religions Around the World*

Connected By Sorrow

The person who shows understanding of your sorrow may be closer in spirit to you than your family is.

After your death, I quickly began to realize which of my friends took the time to understand my loss. I cannot say that my family has been the most supportive, although I know in their own way they try. It seems to me that the people who understand what I am going through the best are those who have also experienced loss. People are connected by sorrow. Sorrow is lessened by spending time with others who know the pain of loss. I have decided to be the kind of a person who will meet someone who is grieving and say, "I am sorry for your loss. I know how much you hurt inside." Then later, I will explain to the person the deeper understandings that may be gained when experiencing the death of, and continuing to communicate with a loved one in another world. I hope I can make a difference for someone else who is grieving.

One of the tasks of true friendship is to listen compassionately and creatively to the hidden silences. Often secrets are not revealed in words. They lie concealed in the silence between words or in the depth of what is unsayable between two people.

—John O'Donohue in
Anam Cara: Spiritual Wisdom of the Celtic World

Making Contact

You do not need to be a saint to make contact with spirits. Becoming good at removing one's attention from every-day life is the key to communication with people in the world beyond. Drumming rhythms are known to alter consciousness and improve access to the world beyond. Singing bowls can be helpful in directing your mind to turn inward and be present to a spiritual place of being.

> *I light a candle and play music. Voices chanting, drums drumming cause me to settle down and look inward. My being is overtaken by something bigger than myself. I feel as though I am being held in God's arms.*

By "spiritual" we mean those aspects of human experience that reflect a transcendent quality, e.g., an encounter with God, a feeling of unity with all humanity, a connection with life in general and with the universe's creative processes.

—Alberto Villodo & Stanley Krippner in
Healing States: A Journey into the World & Spiritual Healing and Shamanism

Lessons From Nature

Nature offers lessons. We understand the springing forth and falling down of leaves as parallel messages about birth and death. Like the leaves, we come to see our own lives in the perspective of a season that is ending all too fast.

> *My feet ruffle the leaves that have fallen down. I am reminded that I too will join you when my time comes.*

*Like dewdrops
on a lotus leaf
I vanish.*

—**Senryu** in *Japanese Death Poems*

Presence

Some of us believe in God. Others feel there is a cosmic force in the universe. Some believe we are all destined by fate. Many believe life is a dance with human will and divine intervention as partners.

> *I believe in our relationship. I believe it was meant to last forever. I feel your presence with me always.*

Though we are God's sons and daughters, we do not realize it yet.

—**Meister Eckhart in Matthew Fox's**
The Coming of the Cosmic Christ: the Healing of Mother Earth and the Birth of Global Renaissance

All We Cannot See

Einstein said that emanations exist that we cannot see. We know that a thing such as electricity cannot be seen but is, nevertheless, real.

> *I feel your energy surround and comfort me. Although I cannot see your energy field, I can feel you are near. We are linked by love. Our connection is real.*

He is said to be dead, yet he is still around.

—**Peter Gallagher in** *Tampa Creative Loafing,* **July 31, 2002**

One With Life, One With Nature

We are all energy. Our energy does not exist in isolation. All energy in the world is connected. We are all connected. Previous generations believed in a seamless life. Birth led to death, which preceded a rebirth. The energy from which we are formed cannot be destroyed.

I believe your energy now is in the form of a spirit. Your spirit cannot be taken away from me.

No matter what your body's appearance is on the outer level, beyond the outer form it is an intensely alive energy field.

—Eckhart Tolle in
A New Earth: Awakening to Your Life's Purpose

A Tree, A Rock, Or A Cloud

Many times when someone dies, we who mourn wish we had better loved that person.

> I shall never tire of a walk in the woods. The trees, the moss, the vines inspire me and hold me in awe. I want to be a small part of this design. I will start by caring for plants, one at a time. I do this in remembrance of you.

One of the stories she had read tonight was called, "A Tree, A Rock, A Cloud."
A man in this story said people should begin by loving easier things before they work up to a person. Begin with something less complex, he proposed. Like a tree, or a rock, or a cloud.

—**Ann Tyler** in *Ladder of Years*

Among Us

People go to extraordinary lengths to understand God.

> *I think God is right here within each of us. God is in the love I have for you. God is in the acts of kindness I do for others. God surrounds us every day. We do not need to go on faraway trips to find God. God is among us and in us, through us, and between us. I now understand the other side is not far away. We can stretch our consciousness to reach individuals who have died.*

One thing we know:
Our God is the same.
This earth is precious to Him.
This we know:
The earth does not belong to man.
Man belongs to the earth.
This we know:
All things are connected.
Like the blood which unites one family.
All things are connected.
Whatever befalls the earth,
Befalls the sons of the earth.
Man did not weave the web of life.
He is merely a strand in it.
Whatever he does to the web,
He does to himself.

—Chief Seattle

In Stillness, I Find My True Self

You cannot see yourself when you look into swirling water. Look into a still pool and your reflection is clear. So it is with understanding ourselves. If we spend all our time in the busy, busy world, we will not learn who we are. It takes times of inner stillness and quiet reflection to know who we are.

> *I used to go for rides in the country and see the woods and roadside flowers from my car. Now I leave the car by the road and walk into the woods, bend down to see the flowers and listen to the voice inside me. Somehow, in this sanctuary, I feel I can better hear myself think. Out in nature, I find space for conversation I am unable to share with anyone else. I do not, however, feel alone at these times. In this stillness, I become part of something bigger than myself. It is like I am walking beside you.*

Hold on to what is good,
Even if it's a handful of earth.
Hold on to what you believe,
Even if it is a tree that stands by itself.
Hold on to what you must do,
Even if it is a long way from here.
Hold on to life,
Even when it is easier letting go.
Hold on to my hand,
Even when I have gone away from you.

—Pueblo Blessing

When We Understand

Many people are able to walk between the worlds of this life and the next. They do so by inviting the sacred community of life ... animals, plants, the earth's elements ... to speak to them.

> *When I am out for a walk, a canopy of trees serves as a backdrop of peacefulness. The light through the leaves surrounds me with mesmerizing energy. I cannot help but look up through the trees at the sky and feel you are there with me.*

All things are the works of the Great Spirit. We should know well that He is within all things: the trees, the grasses, the rivers, the mountains, and all four-legged animals, and the winged peoples; and even more important, we should understand that He is also above all things and peoples; when we do understand all this deeply in our hearts, then we will fear, and love, and know the Great Spirit, and then, we will be and act and live as the Spirit intends.

—Black Elk

Believing In The Extraordinary

Quantum theory proposes that we communicate by extraordinary means with each other not because we are psychic, but rather, because we really belong to a mysterious wholeness in the universe.

> *I believe you and I share a history that cannot be broken by death. We shall always live in each other's presence. For this, I am thankful.*

I once thought love was supposed to be nothing but bliss. I now know it is also worry and grief, hope and trust. And believing in ghosts—that's believing that love never dies. If people we love die, then they are lost only to our ordinary senses. If we remember, we can find them anytime with our hundred secret senses.

—**Amy Tan** in *The Hundred Secret Senses*

Remembering The Good Times

Holidays are supposed to be happy times. Times of light talk and laughter, friendship and family.

> *What remains after a holiday? The memories. Memories are real. I wish to celebrate this holiday by remembering good times with you. I want the people I share holidays with to not forget you were once here, too.*

I still miss those I loved who are no longer with me, but I find I am grateful for having loved them. The gratitude has finally conquered the loss.

—**Rita Mae Brown**

Speaking Your Name

These days we talk so little about death. Most times, we do not know what to say. We have been socialized to convey specific words of consolation at funerals. But beyond the funeral, we are woefully lacking in knowledge about how to proceed. Often we are afraid at holiday gatherings to say the name of a lost loved one in fear that we will dredge up feelings we don't know how to handle. Consequently, during the holidays, when the pain of those who grieve is especially soul-wrenching, we are quiet. We need a nudge to even know if it is all right to mention the name of the deceased.

Understanding all this, it is important that those who have lost a loved one and are grieving lead the way so guests know it is okay to talk openly about the person who died.

> *If I want to talk about you—to hear your name spoken—I will tell my guests so. There is so much about the holidays that I associate with you. I picture your face. I remember your voice. I will say your name. I will talk about you during the holidays. I may show pictures of you. My company will then understand that they can talk with me about you. I find great pleasure in the moments when you are remembered.*

You shouldn't just visit with dead people, you know," she said, like telling me some fact of science. "You've got to pay attention to all of them. It helps them rest. Living people remembering them is what they like."

—**Ann Patchett in** *Taft*

Finding You Still

After loss, grief may overwhelm a person. The person has to reclaim life and go on. This is not to say the lost loved one is left behind. Rather, the person who grieves carries that loved one within them throughout the rest of their life.

I take a step at a time into the outside world. Celebrations are hard for me. I would feel guilty if I enjoyed life too much. I know I must go forward and reclaim participation in life's celebrations, for my sake and for the sake of all those whom you loved so dearly.

Will I ever get her back? No. But by loving me the way she did, my mother taught me that if I look wisely, if I'm attentive and careful, considerate and openhearted, honest and unafraid, it might be possible to find even more of her than I ever had.

—E. Minot

Often Scared

When you ask for help, you let people know you are fragile.

We are approaching the one-year anniversary of your death. I see it ahead of me and I am scared. How will I be on this day? I will come to your grave for sure. Will I break down and cry? Probably I will. I am having a hard time holding tears back right now. Please send me some strength that I may comfort others who also love you.

Death opens unknown doors.
It is most grand to die.

—John Masefield in *In Search of the Dead*

Missing Piece Found

The spirits of all we have loved flow through us.

> *I come across a new situation and find myself stopping and asking what you would think. And then I laugh to myself, for all this wondering confirms that you have stayed with me. Your presence in my heart and mind are a miracle for which I thank God.*

There is a soul force in the universe, which if we permit it, will flow through us and produce miraculous results.

—Gandhi

Notes

Completion of these writings underscores my belief that there is a place where we connect, not just on a human level but on a spiritual plane.

The person who grieves can be transformed by death. Much like the deceased who progresses on to being a spirit, the loved one left behind finds, often for the first time, the spirit within—the essence of their being.

I have to believe that when the Divine made life, He also divined death for a very good reason. Death allows us to take off our masks and be who we really are.

To fully love one another as we are, with all our faults and erring ways, is the ultimate work for which life prepares us.

—Susan L. Schoenbeck, MSN, RN

Susan L. Schoenbeck

Susan Schoenbeck has been a nurse for more than forty years, working in ICUs, emergency rooms, long-term care facilities for the elderly, and group settings for the developmentally disabled. She has taught PN and RN nursing programs and has mentored graduate students. Her work has been published in many peer-reviewed journals. In her books, *The Final Entrance: Journeys Beyond Life* and *Near-Death Experiences: Visits to the Other Side,* Schoenbeck reports experiences of patients who had out-of-body and near-death events. She has received the Universal Voice Award and the Ron Taylor Excellence in Teaching Award.

Schoenbeck grew up in Wisconsin and lives in Portland, Oregon, where she teaches nursing at Carrington College. She is an oblate of the Holy Wisdom Monastery, which follows the Rule of Benedict. She is a past president of the Madison, Wisconsin, chapter of Sigma Theta Tau, a national honor society for nurses, and a member of the International Association for Near-death Studies.

Index

Made in the USA
Lexington, KY
11 March 2014